Utopian Literature

Advisory Editor:
ARTHUR ORCUTT LEWIS, JR.
Professor of English
The Pennsylvania State University

Eden of Labor;

OR, THE CHRISTIAN UTOPIA

T. Wharton Collens

ARNO PRESS & THE NEW YORK TIMES
NEW YORK • 1971

Reprint Edition 1971 by Arno Press Inc.

Reprinted from a copy in The Pennsylvania State University Library

LC# 79-154435
ISBN 0-405-03518-7

Utopian Literature
ISBN for complete set: 0-405-03510-1

Manufactured in the United States of America

See Page 207

MONOGRAM OF POLITICAL ECONOMY

Shewing the science as founded on present legislation and customs.

F. Bourquin Lith.

EDEN OF LABOR;

OR,

THE CHRISTIAN UTOPIA.

BY

T. WHARTON COLLENS,

AUTHOR OF "HUMANICS," "THE HISTORY OF CHARITY," ETC.

And Jesus beholding said to them: With men this is impossible;
but with God all things are possible.—MATT. XIX. 26.

. . . . without me ye can do nothing.—JOHN XV. 5.

PHILADELPHIA:
HENRY CAREY BAIRD & CO.,
INDUSTRIAL PUBLISHERS, BOOKSELLERS, AND IMPORTERS,
810 WALNUT STREET.
1876.

PHILADELPHIA·
COLLINS, PRINTER,
705 Jayne Street.

PREFACE.

To-day, I receive a letter from the publishers, who say they are impressed with the necessity of a Preface, which is not with the copy. They ask for one; and I hasten to comply with their request.

I can think of no better Preface, than a brief statement of the design of the work the reader is about to peruse.

It resolves itself into two points.

To carry to legitimate and ultimate consequences, the fundamental principle admitted by all political economists, viz., "Labor is the real measure of the exchangeable value of all commodities and services." A plan is proposed for a practical application of this principle.

To show that the principle and its application rest, still deeper, upon the rights of God, and the law of *neighborly love* pro-

pounded by our Lord Jesus Christ; and,
therefore, that in his name only, and by the
self-denial which that name implies, can this
law, with its blissful operation, be realized in
this world.

I have attempted to develop these two
points in the form of a narrative; and have
placed the scene of imagined events of that
narrative, in the world before the Flood.
In doing this, I found it difficult to observe
a due proportion between theoretical dis-
cussion, and the requirements of a concrete
relation of the circumstances which I suppose would take place from the realization
of the temporal reign of Christ. I fear
there is too much about the theory, and
too little about what one might imagine
would be the actions, events, and state of
society, to which the application of the
theory would give existence and body. I
could not remedy the defect without producing a much larger and a too costly book,
though it would perhaps have been more
entertaining.

The reader will not fail to see that the history of Nodland, which follows that of the

Eden of Labor, is an appropriate counterpart. It is an exposition of the known effects of the *selfish* principle which has prevailed in the world, but which the name of Jesus will necessarily overcome.

Towards the end, the appropriateness of the "Introduction" will, I hope, be appreciated by the reader. If he is a working man, he will certainly *feel* how rest of mind and body is happiness; and be glad to understand *how* these may be procured, by diminishing, instead of increasing, the excessive toil and anxiety to which he is now subjected. The Postscript and Appendix will be found useful in this respect.

T. WHARTON COLLENS.

New Orleans, 16th January, 1876.
　　Feast of the Holy Name of Jesus.

CONTENTS.

INTRODUCTION.

PAGE

An Essay on Happiness, or Edenic Peace and Rest . . 13

CHAPTER I.

God's Share and Man's Share of Values 37

CHAPTER II.

Adam 47

CHAPTER III.

The Reductions; their Currency and Exchanges . . . 57
Labor-time Measure of Value 66

CHAPTER IV.

Reductionism, its Operation and Effects 68

CHAPTER V.

Other Effects: from Skill, Co-operation, Abundance, Commerce, etc. 77
Formula of the Reductionese Currency 89

CHAPTER VI.

Personal Service and its Reward 90

CHAPTER VII.

PAGE

Nodland; its Landlords and Tenants 113

CHAPTER VIII.

Mines, Machines, Wages, Money, and Finance . . . 126

CHAPTER IX.

Caste and Oppression; War and Conquest 140
    Reign of Enos 140
        Schedule of Castes 141
            First General Division: Lords and Gentry . 141
            Second General Division: Independents . . 143
            Third General Division: Vassals . . 144
            Fourth General Division: Wagemen or Serfs . 145
            Fifth General Division: Outcasts . . 146

CHAPTER X.

Degradation and Reaction 160

CHAPTER XI.

The Deluge of Sin and Death 173

POSTSCRIPT.

New Eden, or How to be Happy on Earth 192

APPENDIX.

Explanation of the Monogram 207

THE EDEN OF LABOR.

INTRODUCTION.

AN ESSAY ON HAPPINESS, OR EDENIC PEACE AND REST.

Ask the philosopher, the moralist, the politician, the economist, or the sociologist, what practical end or result he expects from all his researches and meditations; and if he knows what he is about, he will answer: I aspire to happiness; happiness for myself, happiness for all. The man of small intellect and selfish feeling will seek his own happiness, distinctly and independently, dismissing all care or consideration for the happiness of others or of the State; but enlarged minds, seeing that there is no severance from society, know that the only avenue to private happiness is through public happiness. Hence, they posit the general question what is happiness, and its corollary, what would be the happiness of the State? To answer these questions they ransack all history, all literature, all science, the world. They take great pains and perform much fruitless labor, which might have been saved by doing what ought to have been obvious to a Christian believer. They should have gone at once to *the beginning* of all philosophical truth, the first, second, and third chapters of Genesis; and, with the help of the church, meditating on those chapters of Holy Writ, they would have found a fundamental answer to their question.

Indeed, on this, as on every other question of civil or domestic polity, the replies of the Bible will always be found infinitely more profound, satisfactory, and

2

practical than those of philosophers, moralists, and jurists, who have preferred to trust in their own short-sighted wisdom, or in the speculations of Socrates, Plato, Aristotle, and their successors in Greece, Rome, and Modern Europe.

In their writings and those of their apish admirers, we frequently come across *doléances* on account of their inability to define happiness, their ignorance of what are its proper constituents, and the impossibility of ever attaining it in this world. If they ever offer to say wherein true happiness consists, they not only disagree but every one delivers himself of some vapid sentimentality. Thus each according to his fancy, thinks he sees happiness in the gratification of his own peculiar desire such as it is at the time he writes, and none are able to state a general and at the same time *specific* term, denoting the universal and essential condition of happiness . . . a term which each of us would be willing to accept as the true name of a state of happiness. If asked in what happiness is to be found, what confers it, their answers are: Riches, Glory, Power, Virtue, Retirement, Competence, Gastronomy, Wine and Women, Farming, Books, Shady Groves, Scenery, Sport, Music Festivals, Palaces, Friendship, Love, Piety, or other things too numerous to mention. The majority seem to be in favor of Content; but what will afford contentment? They do not perceive that they have only substituted another word for happiness, reminding us of the lines of Pope:—

> "Who that define it, say they more or less,
> Than this: that happiness is happiness."

We want a definition that points to something we can identify as the substance of happiness. We want an objective point, determining its location—a beacon guiding us to the entrance of its empire—a sign practically useful to all of us in our search and pursuit—a precise test, universally applicable.

Turning, therefore, to the Bible and to the time

when it tells us there was happiness on earth, and seeing what made man and woman happy then in Eden, we are able to say :—

The happiness of man is in REST of mind and body: the happiness of the State is in Peace, because Peace is the rest of the State. Thus the happiness of persons and States consists in rest and peace.

"The Garden of Eden." Eden means pleasure or delight. It means happiness: a garden of happiness. In this garden grew "every tree that is pleasant to the sight and good for food;" and here also was the "tree of knowledge of good and evil; and the Lord took the man and put him in the garden of happiness to dress it and to keep it; and the Lord God commanded the man saying: Of every tree of the garden thou mayst freely eat; but of the tree of knowledge of good and evil, thou shalt not eat." (Gen. ii. 15, 16, 17.)

For disobeying this *single* restriction Adam, among other penalties, was sentenced to this : "*In the sweat of thy face shalt thou eat bread*" (Gen. iii. 19); and Eve to this, "*In sorrow* shalt thou being forth children." (Gen. iii. 16.)

Thus it clearly appears that the happiness of man during his primary state was compounded of three conditions:—

First. INNOCENCE, or inexperience of any *practical* distinction between God's will and human will.

Second. OCCUPATION, without toil; without necessary or fatiguing labor.

Third. EXEMPTION FROM SORROW, or distress of mind.

The first of these conditions, if it is taken in an absolute sense, can never be reinstated. There is no hope of ever regaining paradise by returning to moral ignorance or insensibility ; for *knowledge of good and evil cannot perish*. It is indelible. It descends of necessity from Adam and Eve to their children in every generation. It is presented to us perpetually; and we are ever called upon at our peril to use this knowledge righteously. "See, I have set before thee this day, life and good, death and evil." (Deut. xxx. 15.) The problem now is to re-enter Eden by means of this very knowledge, rejecting the evil and choosing the good. Christ and (through Him) willing Innocence, are the only substitutes for the unhatched conscience of the Man of Eden.

Nevertheless in view of a minuter study of these conditions of happiness, and of their possible service in founding happy society and good government, let us try to form a mental picture of this Man of Eden —to see in imagination his mode of life in his delightful abode.

To do this we must conceive of a state of the world antecedent to commerce, art, and even obligatory labor; and before anything had acquired a value or price.

Suppose, for argument's sake, that Adam and Eve, according to the first of all divine precepts, had increased and multiplied; and had not partaken of the tree of knowledge of good and evil; and that they and their children had continued in their blissful ignorance of sin, among spontaneous and bounteous orchards—what then would have been the life of man?

Man, wholly unacquainted with even the primitive way of making clothes, and unconscious of nakedness, would have inhabited only the regions where the climate was not too rigorous for his nude body, though we may assume that his skin was tough and not over-sensible to heat and cold. Wandering, as he listed, to gaze from the hill-tops, the plains, or the sea shore on the beauties of God's creation—wading or swimming the brooks and rivers as he rambled— reclining at noon under the thickest branches of gigantic and fruitful trees—beholding, with reverential wonder that masterpiece of heavenly art, the sun when it rises at morn, passes the zenith at noon, and goes down at eve—contemplating the starry blue at night, in devotional ecstasy—regarding the ever-

changing and ever-glorious spectacle of the firma
ment, with its sublime and beautiful phenomena of
tinted clouds, refreshing rains, boisterous storms; its
auroras, meteors, lights, shades, and prismatic hues
in all their protean splendor, with more exquisite
satisfaction than civilized people would see the finest
theatrical exhibition—looking at the landscape with
more genuine enjoyment than we now feel in scruti-
nizing whole galleries of paintings—listening to the
music of the birds, of waterfalls, of thunder far and
near, or of the breezes in the flowery copse or wavy
forest, or hearing the simple songs of his family and
companions with more heartfelt enthusiasm than we
hear the orchestra and voices of the grandest opera
—thinking of nature's wonders and conversing about
them in the friendly circle, imagination evoking and
tradition impressing on the book of his memory bal-
lads and romances of which the artistic and polished
compositions of our poets are as dying echoes or
fading shadows—smiling upon and even sharing the
joyous gambols of his children on the greensward
or sandy shore—revelling in the rain or basking in
the sun—catching and bestriding the horses that
grazed on ever-grassy plains—sporting in the spray
of the cascades or in the surf of land-girt waves—
pruning with a piece of sharp flint the useless branches
or plucking with his hands the superfluous leaves of
his favorite fruit trees—clearing them of noxious insects or protecting them from the visits of careless
animals—training a vine over the entrance of a cave
he had chosen for his dwelling—clearing a smooth
path from the cave to the cool spring near by—
merely stretching forth his hands or nimbly climb-
ing any tree to cull and eat his fill of the most
savory fruits, never failing to find the luscious re
past at any time of the year—the frugiverous Edenite would have been occupied, it is true; but, like
Adam, would have done NO WORK.

But this is only one of the aspects—an imperfect
one—in which our imagination conceives the Man of

2*

Eden. This aspect is that of Nature, of innocent nature, of nature that has not yet committed the wickedness of which it is capable. But Adam was not merely naturally innocent. He was supernaturally immaculate. His humanity consisted in a soul inherently rational and conditionally holy; but the condition of this holiness had not been violated, and its dazzling purity, fresh from the Creator's bosom, outshone the refulgent rays of its wisdom. While that soul retained its holiness it had the Science of Spirits and felt the sympathies of Heaven. He was majestic and glorious; invested with all the dignity of intelligence and beauty of virtue. We must reverence him, for he was not ignorantly but wisely immaculate. It must have been so; for the world was and still is peopled with innumerable angels, messengers of heavenly grace superlatively wise and ineffably good, each of whom has a special function of perfection to perform, and who, though now unseen to mortal eye, was then audible and visible to the yet untarnished senses of Man. He freely communed with them. As he *knew* the spiritual sciences and *had* the heavenly virtues, the angels joyfully communed with him; and he joined them in contemplating, understanding, and fulfilling the then clear but now mysterious operations of Providence. Even God himself condescended to speak to Adam audibly. Hence natural science and art as we now know them would have been vanity of vanity to Adam. The experiments of a Galileo, or the inventions of a Watt, would have been trivial and useless to such a creature; for his sphere of knowledge and action was far above these. With the celestial intelligences he observed and studied the mechanism and essence of the infinitely great and infinitely small. His science was acquired by a peculiar process of mind of which only those who enjoy supernatural grace and communion with sinless angels are capable, and this different and grander sphere of knowledge and thought must have furnished different and grander occupations than any of those within the scope and capacity of the natural man. Of this class of Adam's occupations we can form no definite idea, for we have lost the grace, and with it the knowledge and ability it gave; but we know enough to regard and admire the Man of Eden as a *conscious* angel clothed in flesh and blood, and as engaged in the acts and things that interest and occupy the inhabitants of heaven.

This much at least can we say : that by the perpetuations of Edenic life man would have enjoyed all the felicities of personal liberty and intelligent contemplation.

LIBERTY in this: That, surrounded by abundance, untroubled by care of providing raiment, house, and food, he would have been free to exert himself or rest as he felt inclined. 'Twould have been the liberty of the child at play, checked only by willing and reverential obedience to a loved and loving parent. Oh! who does not regret the harmless sports of tenderly protected childhood?

CONTEMPLATION in this: That, without sinking into the perverted and superstitious practices of what pagan mystics and philosophers regard as contemplative life, all men would have lived that other true intellectual and ethereal life extolled by St. Augustin. A life not of phantoms or dreams, but a life wherein understandingly, ingeniously, and really the soul beholds and feels and knows all things intrinsically, and communes as it were with eternal and infinite wisdom, gladly following its dictates and radiating its love.

Though, as we have seen, Adam had no occasion for experimental or applied science—no need, no use whatever for the æsthetical and industrial arts—no occasion to invent ingenious devices for converting matter to sordid uses, his great mind was adequately and delightfully employed. His intellect combined minute discernment and far-reaching scope; exactness of conception and serenity of inference; voluminousness of memory and presence of every possible

association. Hence he could meditate with unfalter-
ing assurance on the immense number of never-for-
gotten facts furnished by his numerous contemplations
of the metaphysical and material worlds. Add to
this his direct and sensible converse with beautifully
immaculate and sublimely illuminated angels, and
we may form some idea of the grandeur and bliss of
his intellectual as well as physical life. How immeasurable then was the least sin, when committed
by a creature so favored and so perfect.

Vain would have been his rest of limb if his heart
had been agitated by envyings, ambitions, and lusts.
Hence it was necessary to happiness that his soul
should also be at rest; that is to say, unagitated by
those worldly cares which accompany or create the
necessity of labor. This rest, this peace of soul, this
exemption from worldly care he found in his love of
the high and pure sentiments and higher science, the
companionship of happy spirits inspired and developed. Hence Adam's soul was serene. No clouds
of despondency obscured, no storms of passion disturbed this serenity of his soul, as he moved majestic,
and wrapped in contemplative ecstasy, over the joyous (flowery and fruitful) landscapes of Eden.

In the supposed case of an Edenite world we must
admit that population was sparse, that the people
had food of the most delectable kind and endless
variety, that this varied food lay on every side in
plenteousness far beyond what they could consume.
Food, being as abundant and as easily appropriated as
light, air, and water, could have had no price, or, as
the political economists say, no exchangeable value.
Every Edenite would have had as much and more
of what his highest conceptions of physical life and
its pleasures demanded.

Hence to form a negative idea of a people living
as Adam and Eve did before the fall, we may com-
pare them with ourselves, and conceive their society
as having hardly any or none of the things we now
esteem as most agreeable. They could have had no

fishing, no hunting, no agriculture, no herdmans-craft, no manufactories, no commerce, no husband-men, no shepherds, no mechanics, no merchants, no plantations, factories, ships, railroads, banks, money, or any medium of trade. They could have no pro-duct of labor, no artificial thing within the whole range of art, from the stupendous pyramid down to a pin or a button; and all this simply because they did NO WORK.

Would this be happiness?

Most certainly it would.

We cannot doubt it; for we have the assurance of Holy Writ, that it was happiness. The very name of Eden adduces the fact; and Isaiah alluding to it says, "Joy and gladness are found therein, with thanksgiving and the melodious voice of praise." (Is. li. 3.)

In the Edenic commonwealth there could be no riches and poverty, no filth or crime, no laws, no police, legislators, princes, armies, nor any pestilence, famine, or war; for these are the results of the struggle of men to escape labor, the immediate and temporal punishment of sin Wonderful! every effort to avoid the penalty has multiplied sin, the horrors of sin and the intensity of labor. The moment man from necessity or his personal comfort bestowed labor on anything, he created value, price, and ownership; and these entailed on the world an ever-recurring cycle of miseries: rapine, slavery, monopoly, caste, fraud, war, conquest, and every other iniquity.

Strange, however, instead of envying these Eden-ites, we are inclined to pity them as suffering extra-ordinary privations. We forget that "if ignorance is bliss 'tis folly to be wise"—that to long for the flesh pots of Egypt we must once have known them —that there can be no privation where there has never been even a suspicion of other comforts than those we enjoy—no unhappiness when our present condition affords all we are able to imagine as un-alloyed good. Moreover, we should remember that if Adam partook not of the agreeable and useful products of art *we* now know of, *he* knew nothing of Avarice, that insatiable dragon whose heads are Profit, Rent, Usury, and Hiring. He had none of the cares, troubles, envyings, longings, disappointments, terrors, fatigues, burdens, indigence, and miseries it is now the lot of the men of labor all over this restless world to suffer.

Why do we seek for riches? Because in the background of every dream of riches or power is the thought of *relief from toil.* Call the object of our efforts by whatever name you please : independence, fortune, property, authority, rank—the real purpose, stripped of the circumstances in which we expect to gain it, and of the dress we put around it, is simply this: to be able to have plenty *without work*, and to enjoy it without remorse. We want to enjoy whatever the vanity of our tastes and our advancement in knowledge approve as pleasant—viands, wines, dress, mansion, and equipage; but we want them *without work.* He who deludes himself with the conceit that he is ambitious of office, honors, and the like, only for glory or the good of his country, will, on carefully sifting his motives, find the residuary notion to be that these will procure (through the good-will or servitude of others) *exemption from imperative toil.* Hence all the artifices of finance, speculation, ambition, and of every other oppression of man by man aim at this : that one may have leave and leisure to occupy himself *as* he pleases and *when* he pleases, as Adam could before the fall, without anxiety of mind or weariness of body.

The Edenite had all the pleasures he esteemed as such without the effort and tire of earning them ; and upon close investigation it will appear that the present struggle of all mankind is to get back to this beginning ; but, alas! the same investigation will disclose (1) how (with the gift of knowledge of good and evil) we are left to our own choosing : (2) how,

in making our choice, we mistake evil for good; and
(3) how we have become infatuated with a medley
of things denounced in Holy Writ as "all vanity and
vexation of spirit" (Ec. ii. 2, 14), or as "the cares of
the world and deceitfulness of riches." (Mat. xiii. 24.)
We fail to see that nothing but the fear of God, and
obedience to His commandments, through love and
Christ, and the relinquishment of every vain pursuit,
will enable us to pass the flaming swords of the angels guarding the entrance of Eden. The whole book
of Ecclesiastes is a demonstration of this truth.

What seemingly immense sacrifices are thus imposed, and how shocking, foolish, and absurd do the
words suggesting them sound to the ear. Starting
from the premise that human philosophy and classi-
cal political economy would furnish, how easy it is
to show that no turning back from the greed of riches
and ambition, or from the vanities of the world, is
required of him who seeks for happiness. Fine and
plausible speeches can be made to demonstrate that
it is "*impossible*" for the poor to discontinue working
—working in the service of capital to produce the
greatest possible amount of everything necessary, useful, or sumptuous at the lowest possible cost. I have
heard and read all that has been said in favor of this
view of the subject; but the Bible has convinced me
that the production of the great riches, so much
vaunted in the standard works of political economy,
is a snare to our feet and a thorn to our side, and
that we must seek for happiness *in the opposite direction*.

Hence we must not go towards glory, power, riches,
or lust to seek for happiness, but towards rest.

By rest I mean not merely exemption from physical toil or excessive bodily labor, but also exemption
from the harrowing pangs and raging fury of the
passions. The violent antagonisms of the passions
torture and rack our souls: disdainful pride, consuming anger, pallid fear, skulking shame, pining

love, rankling jealousy, wan envy, withering care, piercing sorrow, and grim despair—

> . . . . those vultures of the mind
> Its web with labors tear.

He whose bosom is thus torn is deprived of rest—
Rest of Body :
Tranquillity of Mind :
Peace of Society.

This is the summary of happiness according to Scripture. All men who do not despair. travel in search of *these three things in one ;* and many who have lost all hope of reaching the goal, in this world, are consoled in the thought of attaining it beyond the grave—in the resurrection.

What did the Lord promise the Israelites if they obeyed his law in the land he gave them ? REST. (Ex. xxxiii. 14; Deut. xii. 9 ; xxv. 19 ; Jos. i. 15.)

What did he promise them in Babylon, and what now on the same terms? Return and REST. (Is. xxx. 15; Jer. xxx. 10.)

What does Christ say his followers shall have? REST. (Mat. xi. 28, 29, 30.)

What is the grave to those who die in the Lord? REST. (Job iii. 17, 18; Ec. ix. 10.)

What shall they enjoy in the resurrection? REST. (Rev. xiv. 13.)

What is the penalty declared against the wicked? DEPRIVATIONS OF REST. (Ps. xcv. 11; Heb. iii. 18; Rev. xiv. 2.)

Let us contemplate this rest in its social aspect.

Beautiful indeed is the serenity of that unclouded soul from which all evil desires are swept away, and on which the sun of grace shines gloriously ; but still more beautiful is a communion of virtuous souls forming a peaceful society. God is there ! "Behold how good and how pleasant it is for brethren to dwell together in unity." (Ps. cxxxii. 1.) This is the social aspect of rest—it is the "peace of the State." The soul aspires to rest because rest is happiness. *The State aspires to peace, because peace is the rest, and there-*

fore the happiness of the State. Individual happiness
is rest of mind and body. Social happiness is peace
and good-will among men. In this peace and good-
will the body politic has its rest; but the rest and
peace of the State necessarily depend upon the quietude and serenity of the souls of those who compose
society—its members. Where the parts—the members—are disturbed and conflicting, the mass—the
body—must also quake, and may fall to ruin. So the
gospel to solve the problem of social happiness points
back to the individual soul of the man of Eden; and
would restore the individual souls of his progeny to
original purity, and through that purity to peace.
"The wisdom that is from above is first pure, then
peaceable." (James iii. 17, 18; see also, Eph. ii. 17;
Luke ii. 14; Rom. x. 15; Gal. vi. 16.) Thus does the
gospel by these texts and by its whole import offer
peace, as synonymous with happiness. It tenders
first this happy peace to all by the advent of the
Lord—He came to preach peace and good will among
men; and He promises peace to those who observe
His precepts and counsels.

Thus it appears that the word "peace" is at it were
a summing up, in one expression, of all the descrip-
tions given in the gospel, of the practical results or
evolutive effect of the gospel. It certainly excludes
all idea of sin; for sin, and the causes of sin, are the
antipodes of rest of body and soul, or of society.
Who would ever expect peace in a land of sterility
and scarcity, or among those who are envious, tyran-
nical, or sensual? Peace, on the contrary, implies all
the virtues peculiar to Christianity: patience, forbear-
ance, kindness, mildness, humility, meekness, modesty,
chastity, charity; for peace is the fruit of these and
is impossible without these.

The idea of peace also imports the bodily rest of
Eden; for how will the individual soul or the State
be happy when the people are over-worked, driven
by the necessity of soil or climate, or by unequal and
cruel institutions to compulsory, excessive, and un-

3

requited labor? True, the Christian knows how to
bear such wrongs for heaven's sake, and how to offer
the labor that is extorted from him without recompense in this world, as a sacrifice to heaven, but this
very sacrifice implies suffering; and hence, in a
material and earthly point of view, a deprivation of
happiness consequent upon a deprivation of rest.

Why are we patient? We are patient because it
pleases Christ; and it pleases Christ because the fruit
of patience is peace, and peace is rest, and rest is the
promised reward here and hereafter.

For the same reason are we meek, kind, humble,
mild, modest, chaste, charitable, and self-sacrificing.
These are all pleasing to Christ because their fruit is
peace, and peace is rest of body and soul, and rest is
the promised happiness of the just here and hereafter.

It is in society—in the State—that our Lord delights to see this rest realized; for then it is not only
the evidence of the prevalence of the Holy Spirit in
the heart, but also the display of that charity which
is the distinctive and sublimest characteristic of His
gospel. Charity becomes visible, is a reality, only
in society. It is only through the relations arising
in the State that charity can become apparent. Its
root is in the holy sympathy of the members, in their
reciprocal solicitude, in their affectionate regard and
care for one another.

This realization of charity is impossible to the
isolated man. It is possible only to associated man
—to men in society; but what is the final and highest
visible effect of this reciprocal solicitude, of this affectionate regard, of this sympathy of man for man, of this
Christian charity spreading itself through society?
The grand and beautiful temporal result is peace.

The saints love peace. They seek, follow, cultivate peace. They live in peace with each other and
with all men; and thus they have rest. (Is. xxxii. 18.)

So we see the peace of God first ruling the heart,
and then the social body of the faithful. (Col. iii. 15.)

If peace and rest are not in the heart, they cannot

be elsewhere; for they descend from heaven on the heart; and the heart alone is capable of radiating and spreading them over society. Hence if the heart rejects them, they shrink back to heaven. Clearly there is and can be no happiness without this tranquillity of soul and repose of body. We cannot help thinking that exemption from laborious effort coupled with moral innocence, is happiness. The Bible and reason concur in showing that rest is happiness.

But perhaps you object, and reproach me with proposing to banish the sciences and arts from the world. You infer that these would be lost if man sought happiness in rest; but I do not admit the reproach or the inference. I do not propose to banish either science or art; I would not dispense with the measure of study and work they rightfully require. As I have remarked, the temporal consequences of the fall are not revoked in heaven. The decree arresting the spontaneous fruitfulness of the earth, and allowing bread only to those who labor, must stand through all time: yea, even after that complete and universal triumph of the Church—even during that earthly reign of Christ—the millennium.

As I have already remarked, it is now through knowledge we hope to reinstate Eden; but knowledge is not gained by the distressed pauper, driven by relentless masters. Science and invention must be courted at leisure, by diligent but quiet minds, undisturbed by the cares of the world. Hence, somehow or other, there must be some way discovered of procuring leisure to the votaries of science and art. By their own inventions they may shorten and multiply production; create abundance; but abundance does not give happiness without procuring also rest, and, therefore, it is not the abolition of science and art I would propose. On the contrary, I would conciliate them with the procurement of abundance, leisure, and rest, through the triumph of charity.

Here then I posit again the distinction stated in the beginning. Adam was occupied, but he did not work according to the modern idea of work. The word now imports fatigue, anxiety, sweat of the brow. Before the fall, as we have seen, Adam was placed in a garden of delight "to dress it and to keep it ;" but this dressing and keeping must have been an abundantly requiting operation, and an agreeable exercise only ; for real toil, irksome toil, began only with sin. It was from the fall, upon the first act of disobedience, that the Lord God cursed the earth, so that labor and toil became necessary to make it produce. Work is now of divine command, but also work by divine command is again reduced to mere occupation and recreation through charity, reciprocity, and brotherhood.

Indeed even toil is sweet if undergone to help or supply the brethren and to serve God.

It is the motive that has impelled us to acquire science, the object we have in view in our works of art, that curses or blesses them.

There is nothing in the nature of Science and Art to make their votaries unhappy.

We may weigh the planets with Newton, paint Mary and Jesus with Raphael, build St. Peter's with Angelo, find unknown continents with Columbus, sing transcendent odes with Mozart, and yet feel at rest, be perfectly happy. The Sciences and Arts are entirely congenial with Charity and Peace. We may make the good of our neighbor, and the service of God, the object and end of the knowledge we accumulate, the discoveries we make, the inventions we evolve, and the works we perform. In this aspect they are Worship : not toil, but a blessing.

On the other hand, we may make them subservient to Avarice, Usurpation, or Libertinism—make them the servants of every Vice. Then it is they cease to be worship, and become a curse   'Tis then from the motives that induce them and the circumstances that compel them, that the labors of the student and artist are made to pander to selfish vice, and gratify the low taste of a false and godless civilization. 'Tis in this civilization and by its laws that the most iniquitous inequalities and appropriations are sanctioned and perpetuated. 'Tis from the inexorable selfishness and rapacity of these appropriations and sanctions that nine-tenths of the people are compelled to labor for a pitiful subsistence; and that one-half of the work performed by skilled mechanics and common laborers is done only to provide luxuries, trifles, toys, ornaments, tinsel, fantasies, shows, amusements, finery, wines, courtesans, palaces, equipages, and a myriad more vain and useless things for the favorites of legalized Fraud and Force. 'Tis then and from this waste of the bone, sinew, and brain of the toiler upon futile things that the number of those employed in necessary, useful, and good things is diminished, and thereby a greater, but miserably requited labor devolves upon the poor multitude, who, nevertheless, do not escape the corruption and vice of their masters. Their toil, while it is thus excessive, is made galling, bitter, irksome, and harassing by the sordid, the vile, the noxious feelings with which they perform it, and which are induced by the hard exactions and impure example of their hirers. Oh! how bitterly do they hate those who thus extort the sweat of their face without returning adequate recompense. Oh! how they envy their oppressors, and how eagerly would they imitate their rapacity if they had their place. Their overburthensome and unrelenting toil of itself prevent their happiness, since it encroaches upon the rest the natural body normally requires; but there is a deeper cause of unrest and suffering from the sentiments that actuate both the employed and the employer, and drive their souls with excruciating lash and spur, and make them pervert science and art to the uses of selfishness and warring hell, instead of being made, as they might be, the handmaids of loving and peaceful Heaven.

To suit the purposes of hell, the arts and sciences may be made the instruments of unremitting and oppressive labor. To suit the purposes of heaven, the arts and sciences may become the companions and helpers of productive, but attractive and benefi- cent, industry.

Hence in Éden there never was any condemnation of physical science in any department. It was the discovery of the difference between moral good and moral evil through the commission of sin, that was forbidden. The knowledge of physical or corporeal good and evil is harmless to the soul; and hence the forbidden tree was the tree of knowledge of *moral* right and wrong. Another objection is made.

It is denied that the abundance of flowers and fruits, music and song, walks and recreations of an earthly paradise could afford happiness; because the fact is that many, even now, possess all these things and are *not* happy. See the rich man. His table is overloaded with the most savory viands and delecta- ble wines, his halls resound with ravishing music, he disposes of his time capriciously, and some new recreation or pleasure fills each of his days.

This objection and example only show a misappre- hension of the opinions we entertain; and also a mis- apprehension of the sense of Scripture. We did not mean, nor did we say, that happiness consisted merely in no work; but in REST—not merely in physical *rest*, but in rest of body and mind. We made happi- ness depend on three conditions: First, Purity of thought, or innocence of sin. Second, Exemption from toil, but not from occupation; and Third, Ex- emption from solicitude and sorrow. Certainly we did not say or dream that the happiness of Eden con- sisted in the pleasantness of the place—its soft climate, enchanting scenery, and delicious productions. In our theory the substance of happiness does not con- sist in the abundance and excellence of fruits and other things good for the body and pleasant to the senses. *These are not the essence, they are only the means of happiness; the means of rest and peace;* and like every other means may be imperfectly used, wrongly applied, or wickedly abused. For instance, who does not know that a man may be indulging in a succession of variegated luxuries, recreations, and other apparent pleasures—have and enjoy palaces and feasts, and not be *at rest;* not be freely and truly doing what he would like to do; but, in the midst of his revelry, be really a slave of others, of fashion, or of raging passions? Driven by vanity he may be striving to earn the praise of the world, goaded by ambition he may be struggling to establish his influence, or he may be a mere victim of vice. We know enough of all these cases to be able to declare that the leisure and pleasure they display are deceptive; that the dressing, decorating, parading, dancing, visiting, dining, racing, serenading, entertaining, promenading, and sight-seeing of the wealthy are not mere recreative occupations, as they seem to be, but real and painful toil. They are laborious. They are compelled by the exigencies of the world to which one has made himself through his own folly a secretly repining and discontented slave. When the rich man throws open his brilliantly illuminated saloons, spreads his luxurious tables, and hires artists to sing and play in his festivities, what is he but the slave of his guests; a sycophantic caterer to their appetites? What has he been doing but contriving to accumulate the means of paying this tribute to the persons whose good opinion he courts, and who have condescended to avail themselves of his invitations? To tell the anxieties and tribulations a rich man suffers in order to give a single feast would fill a volume. What will he wear? What will he provide? Whom shall he invite? What will people think or say? What ridicule or praise be gained? What profit to fame or power? Who will come or who will despise the invitation? These, and a thousand other questions pregnant with mental torture and fruitful of heart burnings, arise. Then when the event answers the questions, oh! what vexations, disappointments, humiliations, and anguish does he not experience? His

amusements prove themselves on trial to be all labor
and trouble; and having been bought they also turn
out to be morally void.   Before and after, as well as
during his entertainment, he has had no peace or rest,
and therefore no happiness.

True it is that without fertility and abundance
(a large surplus of necessary and good things produced easily and quickly), leisure and recreation, rest
of mind and of body, and therefore happiness cannot
be fully realized.   I have already remarked that this
easy gotten surplus of material substance is a necessary means, and only a means.   Possessed of it the
Edenic Man was relieved of the sordid cares of life.
Food and shelter and every other material comfort he
needed were as plenteous around him as air, water,
and sunshine.   Thus relieved and thus blessed, he
was free to live the higher life of the soul—to feast
his eyes as well as his taste upon the works and gifts
of God in nature—to contemplate them through the
mind as well as by the senses—to have intercourse
with the angelic world and be concerned with angelic
works, and thus to enhance the purity and brightness
of his soul.   But what made these give happiness
was the rest and peace they procured.   This was
happiness, because the soul—being free of sins, such
as envy, ambition, avarice, lust, and full of gentleness,
piety, love—enjoyed the Garden without detriment
from contradictions, doubts, anxieties, fears, opposi-
tions, fatigues, or disappointments, and without any
molestation whatever.   The soul of man in Eden was
in that state of exhilarating rest it may feel again
when reconciled, and when, reclining softly in sera-
phic arms, it shall be calmly and steadily lifted with
wide and wafting wings to regions of transcendent
quietude and vision.   Hence, in one word, the end,
the resultant, the substance of Eden, was not its
material riches and beauty, but its rest.

Of this there can remain no doubt, when upon con
sideration of the fact, that for his disobedience Adam
himself was not cursed, but the ground.   Previously,

the ground had only produced that which " was good" .... "all manner of trees fair to behold and pleasant to eat of"; but, when the original offence was committed, God decreed that the earth should "bring forth thorns and thistles to the offender," so that from that time it was necessary for him to "work and toil" to overcome this barrenness. It is expressly said that this noxious tendency of the soil, and the consequent strain and sweat of the body necessary to make it bear bread, was the immediate punishment inflicted for the eating of the fruit of the forbidden tree. The blight and rankness, at once created the necessity of labor, and stinted the reward of the efforts of the laborer, so that, while he strained his sinews, poured out his sweat, and suffered bodily, his heart was also troubled with fear and disappointment. The curse of sterility was purposely to inflict labor, and labor was to be the express occasion of anxiety and hardship; the occasion of unrest and unhappiness.

It would be easy to *trace all the unhappiness of society and State* to this condemnation to labor, and *to the efforts each of us makes* to avert the effects of this curse from self, by contriving *to impose a double task upon others;* but this would turn us from our present train of thought; and, therefore, I will leave the social evils of labor, and the means of correcting these evils, to be considered another day.

" In the sweat of thy face shalt thou eat bread." This is the sentence that no man can escape. If it does not strike him directly, it will reach him indirectly. Vainly, to avoid this penalty, do we wring the sweat of other men, and gather it for selfish purposes into our own reservoirs; the sternly exacted flood will be red with our own agony, and bitter with our own disappointment.

It is evident, from these premises, that there is a labor of body, a labor of mind, and a labor of feelings; that all three are painful and tormenting; that they all come from the same curse; and that exemption or rest from these three kinds of labor is peace.

Hence it is that the Scriptures speak of peace and rest as the same. Indeed, as we have seen, the peace of the saints in heaven is called rest; and so, in the same sense, the rest of the upright man on earth is called peace; God, the author of peace, and Christ, the Prince of Peace.

Hence, in a hundred places in Scripture, besides those we have referred to, do we see that the main characteristic of happiness is rest and peace.

When the angels of the Lord, surrounded by a multitude of the heavenly army, stood by the watching shepherd, and proclaimed the Saviour's birth, what, besides God's glory, did this army of angels sing? They sang of peace. (Luke ii. 14.)

When Jesus sent forth His Apostles, without purse or scrip or shoes, to preach His gospel, what did He enjoin them, when entering a house, first to say? The words of greeting He taught them were, " Peace be to this house." (Luke x. 5.)

What does Christ promise His Church and followers? Rest and peace. (John xiv. 27.) Indeed, His gospel is the gospel of peace. God is not the God of dissension, but of peace. (1 Cor xiv. 33.)

When the reign of Christ on earth shall be established, when men shall beat their swords into plough-shares, and their spears into pruning hooks, and there shall be no more war, the Lord says, *then* " my people shall sit in the beauty of *peace*, and in the tabernacles of confidence and in wealthy *rest*." (Isaiah xxxii. 18.)

If you were to interrupt me to inquire *how* can this promised, this future Eden be set up despite the condemnation to hard labor incurred by Adam and his sons, I might object that this is not the question before us now. The matter on hand is only the definition of happiness, not the discovery of the means of procuring it; but the answer to this second question is so easy and so short that it will not break the connection of my discourse to give it *en passant*. . . . We may be ransomed from the hard labor that we inherited from Adam, as we were from original sin itself through Christ and charity. To speak more particularly: I say the hardships and injustice suffered by the laboring poor would be relieved by the full development and realization of the mercy and brotherhood taught by the gospel and the Church. I mean that these should not only influence private conduct, but infuse themselves into the body politic. That is my answer to your question, and, if you want further particulars, I refer you to the priest, who will easily describe (to any who cannot imagine for themselves) the happiness, the manifold beauties that would be produced, if Christian charity generally prevailed, and also pervaded the laws and institutions of the city and State.

In His paternal kindness, and in correspondence with man's primary aspirations to rest, Our Father best knowing our nature and destiny, instituted the *Sabbath*, that invaluable and heaven-derived right of the poor. By this merciful institution our Father teaches us, by actual experiment, once a week, in what true happiness consists; yet we are so blind as not to generalize the facts of this reiterated trial of happiness; and instead of trying to "enlarge and multiply our Sabbaths" we are ever rebelliously exerting ourselves to break and diminish even the periodical rest of body and soul He has guaranteed to us. How thankful should be the poor that this right of revisiting Eden every Sunday is secured to them by a higher law, acknowledged even by the rich and by the State. Were it not for the warranty of religion, how long ago would the poor have been deprived of Sunday's rest, and have been forced to toil without intermission? How grateful should they be to this religion, and how ready to defend it, even if it were only for the sake of the Seventh day's rest.

The bondholder, that representative monster, formed of all the woes man's disobedience brought into the world, would, were it not for Christ and His Church, abolish the poor man's day. Not daring to do this, the monster and his like, with their courtiers and retainers, have lengthened the working time of the six other days, to extort, as it were, the blood and sweat which had been saved from their unrelenting cupidity, by the institution of God's holy Sunday.

Though the extortioner triumphs for awhile, the success will be transitory; for a heavenly instinct reminds the children of Adam, even through the ages and generations, of long-lost Eden, and points to a new Eden of rest in the future, descending from heaven.

My friends, I hope I have succeeded in telling what is happiness and where to seek for it. My ardent wish is that we may all succeed in gaining the prize, and that one day the happiness of the whole people will be established on the enjoyment of rightful rest, according to the will of God.

CHAPTER I.

And the eyes of them both were opened; and when they perceived themselves to be naked, *they sewed* together fig-leaves, and made themselves aprons. (Genesis iii. 7.)

And the Lord God made for Adam and his wife, *garments of skins and clothed them.* (Genesis iii. 21.)

And the Lord God sent him out of the paradise of pleasure, *to till the earth* from which he was taken. (Genesis iii. 23.)

Of his own free will Adam incurred the necessary consequences of his determination to rely on his private judgment. (Ecc. i. 13.) These consequences were the experience of evil as well as of good; the loss of divine communication or grace; the loss of the tree of life or source of immortality; the loss of the natural abundance, peace, and rest of Eden; the necessity of working for his subsistence.

It is the last particular of these penalties that now engages our attention.

We may imagine that, in its natural condition, the earth would not have produced spontaneously the abundant and excellent fruits Adam enjoyed in the Paradise of pleasure and rest. As Adam himself was endowed with supernatural graces, so was the earth made supernaturally beautiful and delightful to afford him the happiness the state of his soul and body required and merited. Hence, when the extraordinary graces of his soul were forfeited and taken away, so also was the earth deprived of its corresponding and miraculous bounteousness.

It would seem that the whole earth had been blessed with all the favors bestowed on Eden, except one : the tree of life which grew in Eden only. Not merely Eden, but the whole earth, had been made a fitting habitation for the descendants of man perse-

4

vering in a state of holiness. It is natural to think so from the language of the curse God laid upon the soil. (Gen. iii. 17.) It indicates a change; and therefore a change from fecundity to sterility all over the earth. We are prompted to imagine a teeming land suddenly ceasing to afford, at all times, spontaneous fruits, enough for even the support of two persons without labor. From that moment the life of man was made dependent on hard work. From that moment, he had to provide himself, by manual labor with fuel, tools, and implements, by mechanical labor with clothing and shelter, by agricultural labor with food. From that moment there was no wealth but the product of labor; and from that moment starts a series of innumerable crimes committed by those who, *to avoid the burden*—avoid the divinely imposed burden of eating their bread by the sweat of their face—fasten their share of toil, tenfold, upon the shoulders of others.

Nowhere is the fundamental proposition of Political Economy more emphatically stated than in the third chapter of Genesis.

"Cursed is the earth in thy work; with labor and toil shalt thou eat thereof all the days of thy life." . . . "In the sweat of thy face shalt thou eat bread."

This is the judgment pronounced on *all* the descendants of Adam. Woe unto them who evade it. Its perpetual and general enforcement was made a function of the earth itself. There was doubtless some alleviation after the deluge; for the Lord said (Gen. viii. 21): "I will no more curse the earth for the sake of man"; and the very name of Noah (Gen. v. 28, 29) expresses that through him, and mainly by the God-man whose humanity was to descend from him, men would derive "comfort from works and labors of their hands." But what is the precise difference between antedeluvian sterility and postdeluvian fertility, or what is the difference between the amount of labor necessary for production before the deluge, and that required since then, is not revealed, nor was it needful that it should be. It is my belief that labor generally will be alleviated, in proportion as mankind conforms to the moral and social will of God.

1. Certain it is that, now as always, by the agency of fixed laws, God imparts to things a *natural* productiveness and value.

2. Certain also it is that, through the medium of man's strength and skill, God imparts to things a *labor*, increase and value.

While God mercifully bestows (1) *natural* wealth in inexhaustible quantity, (2) *labor* is still necessary to convert it to human uses, and no man is dispensed from work. This is the law promulgated at the gate of Eden, and it still subsists. "If any man will not work, neither let him eat." (1 Thess. iii. 10.)

Thus, there is a dual title to every product of labor. Firstly, God's title to the natural elements it embraces. Secondly, man's title to the labor he puts into the natural elements to make them fit for use or pleasure.

God has always reserved His title to the natural part, and bestowed title to the labor part, on those only who have added that labor part.

"Behold the heaven is the Lord's thy God, and the heaven of heavens, the earth and all things therein." (Deut. x. 14.)

"The earth is the Lord's, and the fulness thereof: the world and all they that dwell therein." (Ps. xxiv. 1.)

"The silver is mine and the gold is mine, saith the Lord of hosts." (Hagg. ii. 8.)

"All the beasts of the woods are mine, the cattle on the hills and the oxen. I know all the fowls of the air, and with me is the beauty of the field: . . . the world is mine and the fulness thereof." (Ps. l. 10, 11, 12.)

"There is nothing better for a man than that he should eat and drink and that he should make his soul enjoy good *in his labor.* This also I saw that it was from the hand of God." (Ecc. ii. 24; v. 19.)

"Blessed are they that fear the Lord, and walk in His ways; for they shall eat *the labors of their hands;* they shall be blessed, and it shall be well with them." (Ps. cxxviii. 2.)

"He that heapeth together riches by usury and unjust gain, gathereth them for him that will be bountiful to the poor." (Prov. xxviii. 8.)

"He that oppresseth the poor to increase his own riches, shall himself give to one that is richer and shall be in need." (Prov. xxii. 16.)

"Masters, give your servants that which is just and equal, knowing that ye have also a Master in Heaven." (Col. iv. 1.)

Political economists, speaking in the name of natural reason, make the distinction of values I have pointed out. They discriminate between natural value and labor value. They denote the one as inherent, and the other as imparted.

By so doing, they establish a principle—a fundamental principle—of political economy; and, of course, one would expect to see them make important deductions from it, and propose to carry it into some practical effect. The least they were bound to do, was to keep the distinction in mind, when reasoning on the questions they attempt to solve; for they acknowledge it as a primary and universal fact, in their science. But, on the contrary, after stating the duality of value, they hardly take any further notice of it—make no more use of it than if it did not exist. They soon ignore both titles, that of Heaven and that of labor. (1) They give no force and effect even to the tenure *in common,* which they acknowledge is vested by natural law in all men, to all things that remain unchanged by labor; and sanction the reduction of even these, to individual ownership, without labor. (2) They are regardless of the question of how much work there is in a product—how much work is consumed in converting natural things to human uses; and they make the laborer's title and reward dependent upon the artificial and exorbitant —unequally and iniquitously established—value of gold and silver, besides the ruinous and oppressive effects which usury, competition, and monopoly have upon wages, and on every other compensation for labor.

Their first proposition is: labor *adds* value to natural things; their second, following closely on the first, without pretence of inference, is: labor is the *sole* cause of value—the sole producer of wealth, or all wealth is from labor; their third, without debate or hesitation, is: persons individually may acquire and have acquired a private and perpetual ownership in things labor has never touched; and their fourth, derived from the right of the strongest, is: all values and prices, those of labor included, must depend on competition, on relative desire or necessity, and on the monopoly of coin, or of currency representing coin, that symbol and perpetuation of barbaric captures, usurpations and slaveries, and of all other monopolies.

In due order, I will show *how*—after the bodies of men and the land they lived on were confiscated by force, and after the reward of labor was reduced by compulsion to scanty subsistence—gold and silver became the ransom which the powerful preferred to demand for their spoils; and how thereby coin came to embody, and still embodies, every spoliation of fraud and power; how it was and is thereby raised many times above its real and honest value. I defer the consideration of this collateral point in order to pursue the main course of my reflections.

The political economists, having, in the way I have stated, reached the point of accepting relative desire or necessity as the regulator of value, are at their ease; for they have descended, from the height of principles, to the level of the established customs and well-trodden ways of the world. Mammon reigns over the world; and they, as loyal subjects, pro-

4*

pound and eulogize his laws. It is no longer God and labor nor even labor without God; but simply *appropriation* and exchange, as regulated by arbitrary legislation, that they now consider and explain.

In their theory, labor itself is assimilated to property, regarded as merchandise—bought and sold—made subject to all the circumstances and laws of demand and supply; of capital, seeking the largest profit; of necessitous competition between workmen; and of all the other circumstances that affect the possession and transfer of property. In their eyes human labor has no characteristic, no dignity, no merit to entitle it to other or higher rights than the labor of cattle, machinery, or coal. The relation of brotherhood (which should invest human labor with a sacred halo; and cause it to be esteemed, respected, and rewarded as an act of communion between associated equals bound to love one another) is wholly forgotten.

Adam Smith, in the fifth chapter of his first book, says: "Labor is the real *measure* of the exchangeable value of all commodities."

In this *one* short sentence he expresses the double truth I have pointed out; for, labor being the *only* measure of exchangeable value, men when making exchanges have no right to demand any price or part of price for the natural qualities of the things to which they have added their labor. I might take Smith's proposition for my motto, for he declares, in effect, that there is no exchangeable value, but that which is measurable by labor; and it must be conceded that natural things cannot be thus measured. What UNIT *of labor* is there to measure the value of yon shade tree, this fruit tree, that fall of water, that tract of wild land, or the first nugget of gold which the millwright of California picked up? But though Smith wrote the words, and though they have an immense import and pregnancy, he does not stop an instant to consider them. He fails to deduce even one of the many wholesome and beautiful consequences that would flow from the application of the grand principle he enunciates. In his very next passage, he indicates that, somehow or other, labor has ceased to be a standard of value, has ceased to be the real measure, is not recognized as a medium of comparison or of exchange, has itself become mere merchandise, and has become subject to the master-ship and "command" of those who do not labor. He immediately shows that he will treat the natural value as increasing the measure and purchasing power of labor value. He surrenders at once the natural value to labor; but, not content to let it enjoy this accretion, hands over labor itself to the lords or capitalists who have reduced it to the servitude of wages. Indeed, on the next page, he says: "But though labor be the real measure of the exchangeable value of all commodities, it is not that by which their value is commonly estimated." Then he shows how exchange-able value is, now-a-days, vaguely and variably esti-mated by comparing the quantity of one commodity with the quantity of another. That such is the fact is, alas! too true. Practically, the principle that the exchangeable value of commodities is the quantity of labor they contain is not at present, and has not been since Adam was laid in his grave, carried into effect. No doubt the days and hours a poor man has consumed in producing a commodity, have always vaguely suggested, *to him*, the thought that it *ought to be* proportionally valued by that labor, but, since Adamic times, this only equitable rule has never been commonly observed, or even acknowledged, be-tween men transacting barter or sale. Everywhere, for ages, labor value has been left behind, to look forward to the degrees of esteem men diversely and relatively entertain, or the want they suffer, for dif-ferent commodities. Capital holds the commodities which labor, at low wages, has produced; and capital sells them back to the laborer himself, at usurious profit. The workman is made to pay a premium on his work to the idle looker-on.

The great crime of capital is that it does not

merely appropriate natural agents to use as recipients
of labor, but makes them absolutely individual property, arbitrarily invests them with an exchangeable
value, and demands a price for their redemption.

Thus meditating on the duality of value, and the
character of human labor, one day I put to myself
the two questions : (1) What would be the effect if
political economists faithfully and strictly deduced
their science from the fundamental duality of value
that I have just stated, and which they themselves
affirm ? (2) What would have been the practical
result if this view of value had been actually operative, in determining values in exchange, in assessing the reward of labor, and in preventing men from
exacting any price for the share of God ?

I observed that when I had meditated on these two
questions my thoughts took the form of consecutive
tableaux, that followed, as it were, an historical
order. My mind, of its own accord, went to building
ideal representations, showing the living world acting
under the influence of the dual truth that (1) there
is in all property a natural value which has no price,
for it belongs to God ; and (2) an imparted value
which has a price, for it (but it alone) belongs to
labor, according to labor measured by labor. Considering the necessary consequences of such principles, my imagination evoked the ideal scene of a
social and political state materially different from
that in which we live ; different for the better ;
different by precluding the possibility of many abuses
and wrongs ; different by its insuring the real rights
of labor, and by its procuring merited abundance and
needful rest to every laborer.

(1) By imagination I beheld the Eden of Labor,
and its history. I beheld it as it was when Adam,
after the expulsion, organized it among his children,
and gave it laws founded on the principles he had
learned from converse with the Lord in the Eden of
Rest. I saw its happiness and beauty lasting so long

as these laws were obeyed. The proof of this is direct from Scripture.

Speaking to Cain, the Lord said: "Why art thou angry, and why is thy countenance fallen? If thou do well, shalt thou not receive? But, if ill, shall not sin forthwith be present at the door?" (Gen. iv. 6, 7.)

(2) The construction of the beautiful ideal of a country in which justice was done and mercy extended to the poor, of course gave occasion to conceive *how*, from the disregard of primary right and duty, our present institutions were inaugurated, and how they developed their inherent virus of corruption. I saw how war arose from the general perversion of morality; how conquest introduced slavery, landlordship, unequal exchange, and usury; how moral iniquity consecrated every material wrong in the production and distribution of wealth; and how the empire of the Nodlanders finally spread over the earth, provoking the Lord to destroy it by a deluge.

"He said to Noe: The end of all flesh is come before me; the earth is filled with iniquity through them, and I will destroy them with the earth." (Gen. vi. 13.)

(3) I saw, after the deluge, Babylon and Mammon succeeding Nod, and naturally thought of the possibility of overthrowing them by restoring the Eden of Labor through Christ and charity. Immense difficulties presented themselves to my mind when it tried to imagine or deduce a process, a course of action, the course of events, the evolution of existing causes by which the Satanic system might be supplanted by that of Heaven. Nevertheless, I thought I could, by the help of the promises of Christ, prophesy, in consecutive order, movements and events ending in the complete triumph of Jesus Christ, and the establishment of His k ngdom.

I know I have not the literary talent necessary to write with the grace of style and aptness of illustration that impart pleasure. I am also warned that my space is limited, and that I must, therefore, be brief where I should like to be elaborate ; and often deal only in generalities where I should be glad to adduce demonstrative particulars. But, notwithstanding these disadvantages, I persist in attempting this history, for I regard it as a duty to help to show the way of the poor from the Egypt of excessive and unrewarded work to the Holy Land of rest and abundance.

CHAPTER II.

ADAM.

I WILL begin by considering the principal personage of this history as he came forth from the hand of the Creator, and by noting the state of his mind as it was before Heaven drove him to derive from toil and his own counsel the abundance and peace he had madly forfeited.

Let us imagine a previously insensible lump of clay suddenly formed into a living organism, as Adam was, and endowed all at once with manhood, sight, hearing, taste, touch, strength, emotion, and intellectual faculties; then left at the instant alone and naked in the woods. It is clear, if this had been done to Adam, he would have perished. He was ignorant of everything. Every sight he beheld, every sound he heard, was strange to him. He had never eaten or drank. He did not know what was food or drink—could not distinguish what was fit to nourish and refresh from what would poison or strangle him. He did not know how to eat, for he had never seen any one eat. Feeling hunger, he would not have known what it was, nor how to assuage it; and before he could, by himself, have found out, he would have starved to death, not knowing what was the matter, or how to save himself. Man is not a creature of instinct like the beasts, who, without being taught, do spontaneously what is necessary to preserve life. Man knows the simplest things, even the absolute necessaries of existence, only by experience, imitation, and teaching. Hence it was necessary that Adam should be educated before he could do anything for himself. Without this he could not even have known the use of his own limbs. He had not learned the use of his hands, feet, tongue, and so forth. Though they were parts of himself, they were strange to him. We know, from recorded cases, that persons born blind, whose eyes have been opened by surgical operation, are unable, during a considerable time, to understand the effects and uses of vision. At first the sight of the world affects them as a sort of meaningless phantasmagoria, a chaos of nameless wonders. They cannot determine the relation of place and distance by means of sight. They do not identify the same thing by different senses, but regard any one thing seen, heard, tasted, smelt, and touched at different times and in different relations as different things. They admire or fear without knowing why.

At the moment Adam was made—ushered at once into life a full-grown man—everything he saw, every plant, mineral, beast, bird—the light that shone, the sounds he heard, the sky above, the earth beneath, the waters that flowed, all things without exception —must have been, as he first beheld them, impenetrable mysteries in their aspects and their essences, in their qualities and their uses. How could he, naked and ignorant as he was, preserve himself and live? How discover or invent (in time to ward off death) food, clothes, shelter, and the rest? Like an infant, though larger and stronger, he could not appreciate distance, time, weight, size, form, place, and the relative position of things. He would not know what to think of sounds, nor of what he felt through the sense of touch, and would likely, as it is said infants sometimes do, have stretched out his hand to catch the moon. Can you picture to yourself his utter bewilderment and helplessness? Nothing but a miracle could preserve such a creature, isolated as he was—made before society existed.

Yet, no other rational theory can be conceived that would explain the genesis of man, and his primary knowledge of the means of self-preservation.

Therefore we are not surprised to read that the

Lord God was Adam's INSTRUCTOR and HELPER at the outset of the two periods of his life: the Eden of Rest and the Eden of Labor.

In the Eden of Rest, where he had no need of art, Adam learned of God to study nature and invent words. To this end, God prompted him, (1) to classify things, and (2) give them names. God "brought them to Adam to see what he would call them; for whatsoever Adam called any living creature, the same was its name." (Gen. ii. 19.) So must have been done with regard to inanimate as well as animate nature. (Ps. cxlvi. 4.) To name things it was necessary to distinguish them "according to their kinds." This was an introduction to Science; for the beginning of all science is classification. To name things is to create language; for language begins with names, and proceeds to make verbs to express acts, and the other parts of speech to express the relations of names and verbs. Now, we cannot reasonably suppose that such an instructor limited science and language only to this; for He had made Adam to be the great prototype of human nature, physically, intellectually, and morally; and to live supremely happy, in comparative leisure and heavenly conversation. "Seth and Sem obtained glory among men; but above every soul was Adam from the beginning." (Ecclesiasticus xlix. 19.) The obvious inference is, that the happiness of such a being— endowed with elevated reason and angelic holiness— thus placed, must have consisted—could only have consisted—in contemplating and understanding the wonders of creation, in discovering the hidden forces set to work by almighty wisdom, and in tracing their action as they developed the beauteous aspects of things. The deep and broad mind of the great progenitor qualified him for this, and special grace assisted him, so that we may safely say that, apart from art applications, no man ever had deeper insight into the works of God—no natural or metaphysical philosopher was ever more profoundly versed in the laws

5

and principles that God has set to operate the material and moral world.

> "With him his noblest sons might not compare,
> In godlike feature and majestic air;
> Not out of weakness rose his gradual frame
> Perfect from his Creator's hand he came,
> And as in form excelling, so in mind
> The sire of man transcended all mankind:
> A soul was in his eye, and in his speech,
> A dialect of heaven no art could reach;
> For oft of old to him, the evening breeze
> Had borne the voice of God among the trees;
> Angels were wont their song with his to blend
> And talk with him as their familar friend."
>
> *Montgomery.*

But I need not dwell on this period; for I described
it fully in the preceding essay. What directly engages our attention now is the second part of Adam's
life. So, I pass on to the Eden of Labor.

Sent forth to earn his bread by the sweat of his
face, Adam became, at once, a worker at all trades.
Artisan, tiller of the soil, hunter, fisherman, and
shepherd; the first two principally, the others sub-
sidiarily.

A primary necessity was clothing, to cover his
nakedness, for decency's sake; and to protect his
body from the weather, for health and comfort's
sake. Hence, on occasion of the expulsion, the lesson of the Lord to Adam was to teach him the making
of garments of skin. This introduced VESTITECTURE
and all the arts on which it depends, such as tanning
leather, spinning thread, fabricating needles, dyeing
stuffs, and so forth. Doubtless Adam was also immediately taught to build a dwelling; for it is recorded
shortly afterwards that his eldest son Cain built himself "a city." Thus we have to credit Adam with a
knowledge of ARCHITECTURE. Since he was sent forth
"to till the earth," the Lord doubtless gave him also
the instruction he needed for this purpose. He
therefore knew AGRICULTURE. Without implements,
tillage was impossible. The making of garments,
hunting of game, slaughtering cattle, dressing skins,

and building houses, presuppose proper instruments; and since, a few years afterwards, the forging of *iron* became a separate trade, it is fair to infer that Adam was acquainted with MINING and METALLURGY. Then the house and household imply beds, benches, and other furniture, cooking food, keeping milk and oil, and hence the arts of JOINERY and POTTERY, etc.

That the labor Adam performed was of a polytechnic character is therefore evident. No simpler beginning can be imagined even by an evolutionist. In the present age, even after the growth of numerous population, the peoples who are supposed to be in the Adamic or primitive state do not find it useful to have a separation of trades and occupations. Every man of them exerts every kind of industry for his own subsistence and comfort. We may add, in passing, that among these primitive peoples every man is his own merchant; and therefore that, in the distinct and gain-seeking sense, they do not know commerce.

The idea of some that man begins by being a hunter and fisherman will not bear examination. These avocations would not dispense him from being an artisan to manufacture the needed canoe, traps and snares, hut, and household utensils, clothing, and tools. Fishing and hunting are the most precarious of means for obtaining a livelihood, and none resort to them except under circumstances (such as war or brigandage) that render tillage and herding impossible. If the more regular and productive labor of agriculture naturally presented itself and was safe, he of course entered upon it, in preference, as his principal resource. So, after having been primarily a mere gatherer of spontaneous fruit, the first act of labor or production he must have thought of, even without God's special direction, was the planting of the seeds of fruit and vegetables. It seems plain that man, in face of the palpable lesson taught by God and nature, would not have rejected agriculture for hunting and fishing, which are as laborious, more dangerous, more uncertain, and involve more frequent chances of starvation. Peoples follow these exclusively only from necessity, only when a continual state of warfare drives them from place to place, and makes it extremely doubtful that they who sow shall be able to reap, or when they have been driven by bloody and predatory enemies to lands too barren to be cultivated. Of the truth of this remark history and geography furnish us with many instances.

The fair inference from all the facts is, that, from being first a simple fruit-gatherer, Adam entered upon the period of real labor by undertaking all branches at once, but principally agriculture and its auxiliary arts. Then came the division of labor. Cain, the eldest son, continued to be a husbandman; but Abel, the younger, chose to be especially a shepherd. (Gen. iv. 2.) The next specializations were those of Herdsmen, Fine-Artists, and Metallurgists, as shown in the instances of Jabel, Jubal, and Tubalcain. (Gen. iv. 20, 21, 22.) Afterwards another separate avocation was that of Priesthood; for so I understand the case of Henoch. (Gen. iv. 26; v. 24.) It is ages after this, that we first read of hunting being made a separate pursuit. (Gen. x. 8, 9.)

Hence, it is not overstrained to say that, from divine instruction and the genius heaven had given him, Adam was able so to educate and train his children as to make them adepts in the arts I have mentioned. They were so skilled in preparing skins of animals that their articles of dress, composed of this material, were of the last degree of softness and flexibility, coarse or fine, as needed; and always substantial. Nor were they always plain; but were dyed of many colors, and ornamented to suit the taste of the wearer. Their houses were strongly built to last for centuries, eight or nine hundred years, the life of a man, and perhaps longer. But for strength they did not neglect convenience and beauty. So their homes were well closed against the weather, but high and airy and of beautiful

design. Their ploughs and other implements of
labor were well adapted, and thoroughly effective.
They built market places, houses of assembly, and
temples. To go and come between these, they made
roads, bridges, and causeways. They constructed
vessels to convey produce and passengers on the
deep rivers that flowed from Eden. They fashioned
excellent household furniture and utensils. They
devised machinery, and put up mills and factories.
They found placers of gold and mines of coal and
iron, from which they fed forges and smith-shops
where implements and cutlery were manufactured.
In short, they knew and practised all the arts
modern progress so proudly boasts of; but which
afterwards were lost, and are being now only found
again.

In less than three centuries, they were numerous
enough to thickly populate the wide and far reaching valley Adam had chosen to live in, and which
was situated near the source of the Euphrates. As
the Supreme Patriarch stood at the door of the
house he had built, high up on the gradual slope of
the mountain, at the head of the valley, he could
view its entire length and breadth in one scope of
his vision. Standing there he loved to look upon
the multitude of his children, their habitations and
their doings. The mountains that rose like an
inclined plane and formed the two sides of the
valley, like an amphitheatre, extended lengthwise as
far as the eye could reach, and was covered with
farms. Each farm could be distinguished by the
different shading of the green or yellow of its field,
its buildings in the centre, its copse of woodland
and its orchard. This was so distinct that the sides
of the mountains presented the appearance of an
immense chess-board with gigantic squares of di-
verse coloring, on each of which was placed the
home of a family, instead of a towering pawn or
castle. Higher up, the rocky ridge rimmed the
skies; and down below the wide and flowing Eu-

phrates meandered in serpentine curves. Across
the river, at convenient distances, bridges threw the
span of their arches; and on either bank, not far
apart, were tidy villages or large factory buildings.
In several places majestic temples spread their
domes as if to copy the blue sky above them.
Roads traversed the whole scene in every direction.
In the fields were men engaged in tillage or gathering the fruits of their toil. On the pastures grazed
sheep or other cattle. On the roads rolled carts
and other carriages. The face of winding Euphrates was jotted with deeply laden vessels and light
sailing-boats. The streets of the villages teemed
with busy denizens going to and fro in pursuit of
their various industries. Amid all and from everywhere came thousands of sounds, the hammer of
the smith, the rumble of vehicles, the lowing, bleat-
ing, and barking of beasts, the crowing or chirp of
birds, the hum of insects, the speeches and songs of
men. Life, labor, and music teemed all over the
grand panorama which that beautiful valley presented to the eye. Over all, clearly and genially,
shone the sun, gilding with lustre every prominent
object, casting transparent shadows on surfaces
below, and tinting with every hue the innumerable
and variegated objects that filled up the magnificent
landscape.

To this fair land and industrious people, Adam
had given divinely inspired laws; and over it he
reigned with sovereign authority and parental tenderness. He was the first legislator and king by
virtue of the natural course of events, and by the
special decree of Providence. The people obeyed
him, for they were his children. Every one of them
coming into the world found his majesty and power
unqualifiedly acknowledged and reverenced. They
grew up under his paternal administration and
authority. They were distributed and organized
according to his divinely instructed wisdom. He
was their natural and constituted sovereign.

We have already seen how well he was intellectually qualified for this high office. His moral qualifications also gave him a pre-eminent title to the assumption of this task and dignity.

From the fact that Heaven invested Adam with patriarchal authority, I infer that all necessary knowledge of moral law was imparted to him. Since God condescended to hold supernatural intercourse with him, to teach him practical arts immediately needful for his temporal subsistence, it follows, for the greater reason, that God also instructed him in the maxims and rules indispensable for his moral life. Indeed, on this point there is hardly room for mere inference. We know expressly that, from the Tree of Temptation, our first parents acquired knowledge of the distinction between good and evil, not of mere physical pleasure and pain, as some inconsiderately imagine, but of moral good and evil, which, as clearly implied by the language, consist simply in obedience or disobedience to laws divinely revealed. True, that, by the fall, Adam lost original holiness and several special supernatural graces, of which we cannot now have any exact idea; but he had recently been in communion with angels, and in conversation with God himself. Assuredly he received the revelation of the perfect divine law of morality. God did not fail to teach him the same moral and social doctrine, the same laws and precepts that Christ taught his disciples. All the spiritual wisdom now understood only by Christian saints must have been communicated to him from heaven, and he must have diligently taught it to his children. He necessarily had Faith, a faith as intense as Seth, or Henoch, or any other patriarch or apostle subsequently had; for in like manner his knowledge of God was direct and immediate. Nevertheless, he retained the freedom of his will, was left to his own judgment in carrying out the principles he had learned, and was liable to be pressed and deluded by pride, envy, and sensuality. No doubt he resisted these with great, though not absolute success; for the lesson he had imbibed of the magnitude of the guilt involved in even the least act of disobedience to divine law, influenced him to lead a religious and virtuous life, and carefully train his children to do the same. Of the fact of religious education, we have direct evidence. The sacrifices Cain and Abel made (Gen. iv. 3–5): the one of the first-fruits of the year, the other of the firstlings of his flock, prove they had been taught Worship and its ceremonial rules; and all else that the worship of the true God implies. The terms of the Lord's rebuke (Gen. iv. 6, 7) show that Cain was fully informed of what was Sin, what its consequences, and that he had power to avoid it by self-control. Sum total, it is certain that, even after the fall, Adam was a man of the greatest excellence—a man endowed with the proper graces and dignity of character required for sovereignty, and with the wisdom and virtue essential to a good and great legislator.

CHAPTER III.

HENCE, during Adam's long life of eight centuries after the expulsion, his home and dominions were the Eden of Labor. There was no immediate economical cause for a subversion of justice and charity among his children. In his family, during his reign, the relative rights of God and labor were respected. Indeed, from the pains he took to inculcate and enforce obedience to heavenly derived laws and precepts, the divine right must have predominated. The murder of Abel might raise a doubt of this general fact, were we not told (Gen. iv. 13–16) how, after committing the deed, Cain fled into exile, was torn by remorse, and acknowledged the existence of a law governing society, according to which the penalty of death would have been inflicted on him for his crime, had it not been for the intervention of mercy.

The increase of population during antediluvian times was wonderfully rapid. It proceeded by a triple ratio; for, by reason of great longevity, the number of deaths compared to births, during the first ten centuries, was proportionally few. It is safe to say the population doubled every thirty years, so that by the time of Adam's death the number of human inhabitants on the face of the earth exceeded a hundred millions.

As this rapid multiplication of people went on, the superlative intellect and organizing character of Adam were put forth in adequate proportion. Every thirty years new families segregated from the paternal home, and founded new homes, fraternities, clans, tribes, kindreds, and patriarchates. The first frater-

nity which Adam organized, composed of over one
thousand of his nearest descendants, and the territory they occupied he called a REDUCTION, because
therein he had *reduced* material nature to human labor
and the moral nature of man himself to the will of
God, as he had been commanded to do. Afterwards
he called the territory of a clan a CLANDOM: that of
a tribe a TRIBEDOM; that of several nearly related
tribes a KINDOM; that of a certain number of kindoms, forming a great province, under the vice-
gerency of one of his sons by Eve, a PATRIARCHDOM;
and, finally, all the countries acknowledging his
sovereignty, the SUPREME PATRIARCHDOM.

The fundamental laws the Supreme Patriarch promulgated were: first, the fatherly and absolute
sovereignty of God; second, the brotherhood of humanity; third, the legal equality of persons; fourth,
the title of every man to all natural things, not for
intrinsic or perpetual ownership, but for transient
possession and use; and fifth, on the first four, he
based the commercial statute which was enforced,
during his reign by means of practical ordinances:
"*Labor is the real measure of the exchangeable value of
all commodities and services.*"

But *how* did he manage to apply this economic
principle? What were those practical ordinances?
How could he value the *real labor* blended in a commodity independently of the natural value it comprised? How find the equation of the differences of
(1) time, (2) effort, and (3) skill merged in *similar*
products? How make a like equation of (1) time,
(2) effort, and (3) skill involved in the production of
different commodities? How keep account of the
labor put into *each stage* through which a commodity
passes from raw material to a fitness for final consumption; and of the wear and tear of tools and
machinery, and consumption of materials used in
making up a complete and finished article, in order
that the last workman, and every workman before
him, may have his just reward, no more, no less?

How adjust cases of inequality of *quantity* resulting from (1) natural causes or (2) differences in skill, but involving the same amount of labor? How apply the pure and simple standard of labor to differences of *quality*, such as greater or less beauty, finer or coarser flavor, longer or shorter durability resulting from (1) superior or inferior skill, or (2) from weather, soil, and other natural conditions, but involving the same amount of labor? What must be the *unit* of this real measure, the unit wherewith the labor contained in all products should be valued, and according to which they could, whatever their dissimilarity, be equitably exchanged?

The supreme patriarch easily solved these questions which seem so hard to answer. He succeeded perfectly, because he simply and inexorably adhered to principle or fundamental law. *Nature works for nothing*, said he; and he was determined that for what nature had done gratuitously no price whatever should be exacted.

By close observation, in honestly seeking to find or invent means to the just and beneficent end of securing to labor its just and true recompense, he discovered that, in a given length of *time*, there was a constant AVERAGE of labor and skill exerted by those who converted natural things to human uses. He *analyzed* every work done by men, and found that each kind was *reducible* to particular quantities or tasks, measurable by *time*. For instance, he ascertained that it takes a good and diligent workman just so many days or hours or minutes to clear, plough, weed, or reap an acre of land, or to gather and garner a ton of harvest, or to cut a cord of wood, or hew a rod of timber, or to prepare or cook and serve a pound of food, or weave a yard of cloth, or to write a folio of manuscript, or to cut and sew a garment, or to dig a cubic yard of trench, or to build a house, a fence, a bridge, or other such work, or to make a particular article of furniture, or to grind a quarter of wheat, milk a cow, butcher an ox, churn a gallon of milk, or to render any other specific service. This, even with regard respectively to each distinguishable quality, condition of things, or peculiarity of circumstance. We know that this was entirely feasible from the fact that, in our times, laborers and workmen often do what is called "*piece-work*," and are paid well-settled prices, according to certain specified measures of product; but the price of each piece of work is really determined by the *average time* an ordinary workman must take to do it well. Miners are paid by the ton; masons by the thousand of brick they lay; carpenters by the square; tailors by a special sum for each kind of garment they sew; authors are compensated at so much per line; printers by the thousand *ems ;* there are rates of piece-work in almost every trade or profession. It is true that, in regard to *prices*, these rates are not, *at present*, justly determined; but in regard to measurement of work, *by the average ratio of* TIME *to quantity or quality of* PRODUCT, they are nearly correct.

The examples I have cited should be sufficient; but, if the reader is not yet satisfied, let him consider what farmers and mechanics actually do in this respect.

An experienced farmer can tell exactly how many able-bodied men he must employ to cultivate his land, to raise this or that kind of produce on his number of acres, how many days' work each will or must do to make the crop. In the course of the year, and according to the seasons, he sets them to do a great variety of works. In one season he sets them to ploughing, in another to planting, in another to weeding, in another to reaping, etc. etc.; and he knows that the days of work and their product will come out even; for he has correctly estimated their relation, how much of one is equal to so much of the other. Every day he readily and correctly decides, not only what is to be done, but how much work of each kind can be done by his laborers, and distributes to each man his task for the day without assigning

to any one more or less than he is able to do that day.
One, he assigns to spading and manuring a garden
bed; another, to gathering fruit in the orchard; a
third, to repairing fences; a fourth, to feeding horses
and cattle, and driving the cart to market; a woman,
to milk the cows, make the butter, feed and house the
fowls, and gather the eggs; a number to hoeing the
corn, and he knows, in the evening, by inspecting
the results, that they have respectively done a fair
day's work. This is repeated every day of the year
under a continually changing concourse of circumstances, the employments of one day must materially
differ from those of other days; and, nevertheless, the
farmer is ever able daily to determine each laborer's
task. He sometimes keeps a detailed account of
every hour's work done with specification of its particular nature. He does not fail to correctly foresee,
under penalty of a waste of time or a slighting of
work if he makes a mistake. Hence, it is seen that,
even in the most complicated of industries, every
stroke of work is commensurate with a length of time,
great or small, but definable. An experienced person
might safely contract to manage a farm on this principle for a predetermined annual sum total of cost.
All that is needed to apply this relation is diligent
or habitual observation and comparison, such as any
ordinary man can exercise.

In every branch of mechanics we see the same practicability of this commensuration of time, labor, and
product. In every mechanical business, masters
undertake works by the JOB ; and to do this with advantage to themselves they make estimates of cost.
True, these estimates are expressed in dollars and
cents; but to find this money cost they make schedules
of the number of days' work that will be required.
The house or ship builder, with the plans before him,
is able to make out, not only a detailed list of materials he must purchase, but tables of the number of
workmen he must employ, and of the number of days
and hours each set of workmen or individual will be

6

employed in preparing, putting together the materials, and completing the job The house builder, for instance, employs many different kinds of workmen, common laborers, carpenters, bricklayers, plasterers, plumbers, painters, slaters, stone-cutters, etc. etc.; but he knows the time they will make and the quantity of work they will do in that time, so that he is able to bind himself, under a penalty, to finish and deliver the building in a definite number of weeks, or at a certain date. His furnishers of materials all do the same thing for themselves, and it would be easy to *estimate, in units of time,* every made article or commodity that enters into the job.

These examples are sufficient. It is unnecessary to go the whole round of polytechnics, to illustrate the feasibility of valuing *products* and *services* by the UNITS OF TIME which the labor they involve has consumed, independently of cost in money or of any other thing that might be used as a common medium of exchange.

Any attentive and ingenious man, versed in any art, can see how this method of measuring products and services in the naked ratio of time, can be made equitable and exact in every particular.

Whether there is or can be a just valuation of labor or products in gold coin or in currency representing gold coin, or in corn or any other material thing, is a question which has nothing whatever to do with the standard or basis of value used in the Adamic reductions or Eden of Labor. To understand the reductional standard all reference to *material* measures of commodities, such as corn or other articles of commerce—all relations to coin or denominations of coin, such as dollars, francs, pounds sterling, or the like, must be dismissed from the mind —absolutely eliminated from the idea—discarded as entirely unfit to be made common measures of exchangeable value. No elements must be regarded and admitted in the conception other than TIME, as a measure, applied to labor and its PRODUCTS ; so that each product or service would have exchangeable value only in the ratio the LABOR it contains really and specifically bears to time. Whosoever mixes any other notion with this idea of exchangeable value cannot clearly understand it. Instead of having, for instance, the idea of a dollar's worth of corn, he must form the idea of a *time's worth*—a day, an hour, a minute's labor-worth—of corn. If he does this, then he understands the triple relation of (1) time, (2) labor, and (3) product in the determination of exchangeable value. If he does not or cannot do this, then he does not or cannot understand.

Though it is to repeat, I insist that the idea I wish to impress is not that the amount of labor-time and purchase of materials spent in producing a particular article, and which constitute its actual *cost*, but the labor-time good and diligent workmen ordinarily require to produce the like, out of natural things, which is the legitimate price. The labor-time wasted in slow or bad work is of no account in the estimate of labor-time value.

There is another danger of misapprehension. It is, that some may imagine the Reductional System would (as do several modern theories of labor-exchange) allow individuals, under pretext of personal right, liberty, self-ownership, or the like, to value their own labor at their own price, regardless of its measure in average labor-time product; and, therefore, buy or sell service or products of labor at more or less than labor-time value. To have permitted this would have been to sanction monopolies of natural values, the freaks of demand and supply, the envy of competition and speculation, and other means of extortion which have caused all the economic miseries of the modern world. This would have undone, by one law, what had been done by the other. Thus the principle laid as the foundation of justice and common right would be immediately defeated by any individuals, or by combinations express or tacit. Thus the allowed exception would soon become the general rule. In the Eden of Labor, on the contrary, every infringement of the rule of exchange by the labor-time estimate was reprobated and punished as EXTORTION. The infringement was assimilated to robbery or theft, which are public offences no private person could condone; or, rather, it was likened to the use of false weights and measures, or to the passing of counterfeit money, which no consent to receive can legalize. The strict enforcement of the labor-time estimate was regarded, under reductionism, as in nowise an encroachment on individual rights; but, on the contrary, as the maintenance of the most sacred of those rights, not only of the weak and foolish against the strong, but of public morals, prosperity, and order, against those who would selfishly and absurdly destroy them. Taking more or giving less than standard labor-time value was, under the Adamic rule, an offence against society itself, not to be superseded by any supposed personal right; for there can be no personal right against honesty and equity.

In the Eden of Labor, by a careful, *minute*, and conscientious series of observations, they succeeded in finding the true and exact ratio of every product and service to the average labor-time it embodied. In every *Reduction* there were experienced appraisers conversant with all the principal and petty, all the constant and variable, details of labor, required for the extraction of raw material, and for every kind of cultivation and manufacture. They prepared elaborate tables of the time necessary for the AVERAGE doing of each item or iota of labor in a workmanlike manner. Indeed, in the course of time and practice everybody became familiar, not only with the standard, but with the estimates, and was able to apply them with readiness and certainty. People in general (even children) could tell promptly and precisely how many minutes or hours of average labor there were in any article or service they were in the habit of consuming, or even seeing.

In every Reduction, and at the capital of every clandom, tribedom, kindom, and patriarchdom, there were a public market and corporate stores where any one might deliver acceptable commodities to be sold, and where the price of the consignment was immediately paid or credited to the depositor, on the basis of labor for labor, equally valued according to the method I have tried to describe. Indeed, the consignor was not always required to deposit his product in the public market or store. Most frequently, especially with respect to bulky articles, a more convenient course of business was pursued. The producer merely informed the public appraiser, who was also the public proxy, in charge of the public market and stores, that he had a certain product in his granary, or house, and wished to consign it. Thereupon the public proxy would, either himself or by deputy, go and estimate the labor-time value, for which he would give the producer credit on the books. This at once invested the public proxy with the sole right of disposing of the things consigned. The producer from that moment held them in trust; and if he dared to use, convert, or convey them, he was guilty of embezzlement, and, on conviction, was severely punished. Rarely, or hardly ever, did any one commit the crime. The people were generally honest, and public opinion strict. Besides, from the nature of the case, detection, in a few days, was inevitable.

When any man's product was accepted by the public proxy, he was entitled either to credit on the books for the labor value or to immediate payment in CURRENCY representing that labor value. This currency was issued by the reduction, clandom, tribedom, kindom, patriarchdom, or Supreme Patriarchdom, according as the consignment was made to markets and warehouses of one or the other. It was in the form of bills of credit of different amounts expressed in units and integers of labor-time. It set forth these units in the following table of—

Labor-time Measure of Value.

10 vibrations (or 1 second)	one *stroke* of work.
10 *strokes* (or 6 seconds)	one *dash* of work.
10 *dashes* (or 1 minute)	one *strive* of work.
10 *strives* (or 6 minutes)	one *round* of work.
10 *rounds* (or 1 hour)	one *tire* of work.
6 *tires* (or 6 hours)	one *day* of work.
6 *days* of work	one *rest* from work.

The immediate right a person acquired by taking the notes was that of using them to purchase anything he wanted at the public market and stores, at a price in labor-time ascertained by the same means of appraisement according to which he had parted with his own goods.

EXCHANGES between the reductions and other sub-divisions were carried on through their several public proxies, and at their different markets and TRADE CENTRES, according to a well-defined arrangement. The reductionary proxy was in correspondence, *for exchanges*, with the proxy of their *clandom*—those of clandoms with that of their *tribedom*—those of tribedoms with that of their *kindom*—those of kindoms with that of their *patriarchdom*—and those of the patriarchdoms with that of the *Supreme Patriarchdom* and with foreign countries. A man might order his goods to be sent at once to any one of these trade-centres; but as he could gain nothing pecuniarily by such a step, he generally left them to be disposed of by his own immediate reductionary proxy. By means of their correspondence, and through all sources of information, the public proxies ascertained (1) the wants of their constituents, (2) the markets from which these could be supplied, (3) gave intelligence of the quantity and quality of their own stock, (4) received orders for the goods they had for exchange, and (5) sent orders for the things they required. The grange combination recently started in the United States is being constructed on a similar plan, subject, however, to all the disproportions and other evils of competition, fluctuations of price, credit speculations, a false currency, and so forth. Lieutenant Maury's great plan for reporting the actual products of agriculture and manufactures, already partially carried into effect by the government, is an illustration of one of the means employed in the Eden of Labor, to enable the people to know, all the time, what direction and extension they should give to their industry.

An inferior trade-centre (that of a reduction for instance) *was prohibited by law from issuing its labor notes to the higher ones.* The order observed was this: the reductionary proxy could only issue notes to private persons consigning goods to him. The clan proxy could only issue notes to private persons, or to reductionary proxies consigning goods to him. The same rule was imposed on the entire series of trade-centres in the order of their seriation.

A distinct and peculiar advantage of the reductional system of markets, exchange, and distribution was that fresh products could not be regrated or monopolized, or otherwise kept back from consumption, so that they found a free and immediate way from producer to consumer, and were not lost by decay, deterioration, or waste.

ERRATA.

The Table at page 66 should be as follows:—

1 vibration	is $\frac{36}{1000}$	of a second.
10 vibrations. . . one *stroke* of work or	$\frac{36}{100}$	of a second.
10 *strokes* . . . . . one *dash* of work or	$3\frac{6}{10}$	seconds.
10 *dashes* . . . . . one *strive* of work or	36	seconds.
10 *strives* . . . . . one *round* of work or	6	minutes.
10 *rounds* . . . . . one *tire* of work or one hour.		
6 *tires* . . . . . one *day* of work.		
6 *days* of work one *rest* from work.		

CHAPTER IV.

REDUCTIONISM, ITS OPERATION AND EFFECTS.

As the reductionary proxies were the *immediate* agents of the *original* producers, as they were the beginning and the end of the process and machinery of exchange and distribution, and as the other proxies were only portage and transfer agents between the reductions, it followed that the reductionary proxies and their immediate constituents, the original producers, were the recipients of the final balances of currency, if indeed any such final balances were ever possible. The flow of products was *from* the producers *to* the distributing centres; and, therefore, the main flow of currency was from the distributing centres. The tide or eddy-flow of currency returned to the distributing centres, to be finally cancelled by exchange of goods, which followed the money everywhere to redeem and cancel it. Indeed the distributing centres generally returned produce for produce, instead of paying in currency; but in consequence of the rule mentioned in the preceding chapter, whatever amounts of National Labor Notes were issued from the emporiums found their way in a direction downwards to the reductionary proxy, and through him into the hands of his home contituents, and by them into general circulation. By the play of this system, the reductionary proxy was constantly receiving *transient* balances in this currency; and therefore, generally had on hand as much of the higher order of notes as his constituents had any need for. Hence it was hardly ever necessary for him, or the proxy of any clan or tribe, to issue a local note. Those who had occasion to exact notes of one kind or the other from the public proxy, soon found it necessary to use them to make purchases from or payments to their neighbors, or to bring them back to the reductionary market and store to make purchases there. Thus the National Labor Note constituted nearly the only circulating medium; and it did not require a great amount of these to transact all the affairs in which money was at all needed. The net *movable* wealth and capital of the country consisted in the produce and merchandise consigned to the trade-centres, in charge of the public proxies, subject to the orders of consignors for the things in kind, or to the checks of consignors for the price in money; but for the money there was comparatively no great demand; for transactions between individuals were mostly settled by checks on the proxy; and thus the property on deposit, at the *trade-centres*, passed from one person to the other without changing place, till it was wanted for positive consumption. Hence, the markets and stores in charge of the proxies, and their manner of transacting business operated as a currency bank and storage warehouse combined in one institution taking deposits and issuing circulation, keeping transfer books and giving warehouse receipts, paying checks, and passing book credits from one depositor or consignor to the other. Hence, also, since every one of these transactions, under the system, was necessarily a *real* one, the yearly liquidation came out true and even, and the surplus to meet the exigences of reproduction and future need were always certain, abundant, and available.

One point should be now more clearly stated, to present a more complete and clear idea of the reductional system.

There are several unavoidable disparities in the *intrinsic* value of the results or products of labor and skill. First: The same amount of labor gives different *quantities* of product, greater in one case and less in the other to the average; and this difference is the result, (1) sometimes of skill turning out more than the average; (2) sometimes of soil, climate, and other natural causes developing a larger or smaller product; and, (3) an increased product is sometimes due to both these causes combined. Second: The same amount of labor gives different *qualities* of product according to the influences of, (1) skill, (2) nature, or (3) both combined, which I have just stated as affecting quantity.

In other words, a greater quantity or better quality of product may be the result of, (1) less labor, (2) or more skill.

Now, from these facts, some would be disposed to deny the justice of determining price or value by the average labor-time standard only, but a little reflection will remove all objection.

As to the (1) accessions in QUANTITY, and (2) superiorities of QUALITY arising from *natural* causes merely, they are due to the act of God—they belong only to Him; and no man acquires the right of demanding extra ransom for them. God makes the favored producer, in this case, the custodian and distributor of *His* gifts. Let him give thanks that these have fallen to his lot to be thus disposed of. Let him personally consume all he needs of the abundance and excellence; but to Divine mercy he owes, in return, the duty of selling the surplus to his neighbor by the rule of labor for labor. Moreover, his neighbor owes the same to him, and it will as often happen that his neighbor's products will be as bountiful and as good in one kind as his are in another. If his neighbor's wheat crop be poorer than his, that same or another neighbor's fruit crop may be the finest. The neighbor, who from mere natural accidents, made an inferior crop should not be regarded with an evil eye, nor begrudged the slight increment he would derive from the general average of the production of the year, in the whole country.

The same, and other worse discrepancies happen, with tenfold aggravation, under the rule of total appropriation and absolute ownership of natural blessings, by individuals. I need say nothing of the untoward fluctuations of prices, and the train of other evils caused by envious and avaricious competition and monopoly; for it suffices to point out that the differences in quantity, from natural causes and accidents, happen under one system as well as another, and he whom Providence favors to-day may see that favor withdrawn to-morrow, and extended to his neighbor. The material difference is that reductionism remedies the mishap at once, and equalizes the loss immediately as between partners and brethren. This is the laborer's equity and charity. It is, therefore, not only prudent to reciprocate, and to *insure* one another against unforeseen and unusual circumstances, or even against mere accidents; but, also, it is our duty to please God by distributing *His* blessings to one another in brotherly devotedness and love.

" For I mean, not that others should be eased and you burdened; but by an equality, in the present time, let your abundance supply their want, that their abundance also may supply your want, that there may be an equality, as it is written: He that had much had nothing over, and he that had little had no want." (2 Cor. viii. 13, 14, 15; Exod. xvi. 18.)

As to *skill*, alas! who will complain that the reduc tionism of the Eden of Labor treated it inequitably? Not certainly the skilful *wagemen* of the land of Nod ; for they were paid at first but a small premium over the ordinary workmen of their own craft; and as skilful hands of that craft became more and more numerous, their wages were continually falling lower and lower, till the money one of them was paid for a day's work would not purchase a *fourth* as much as a day's labor-note of the Eden of Labor could command. None of them got the equivalent of his time and skill; for, three-fourths of equivalent was retained as *profit* made out of their time and talent by their employers, and by the usurers, merchants, speculators, land owners, and monopolists, who extorted gain from those very employers. For instance, the printers of Nod were, immediately after the invention of their art, paid very large prices for their work. Their books were, it is true, cheaper than manuscripts, because much less labor was required per copy, but this difference was more than made up by the great number of copies they sold, so that their remuneration largely exceeded that of the skilful manuscript copyers, whom they supplanted. There were few printers then; and these (as all printers are even to this time) were well versed in philology and literature. They wore the dress of the gentleman of their times, and were cordially received into aristocratic society. But, in the course of less than a century, their skill became common, their numbers great, and they underbid each other for employment, till at last the best of them were forced to excessive work, at a rate of wages little more than enough to provide them with the meanest grade of livelihood. Nor did this stop here; for, by and by, even women and children learned to compete with them; and machinery (costing so much that only capitalists could own it) was invented to do their work better and faster than their skilful fingers could possibly achieve.

Nearly the same thing happened to the "clerks." Driven from the business of copying and illuminating manuscripts, they learned printing, or devoted themselves to school teaching. I have told the fate of those who turned to printing. A similar ruin befell the school-masters and professors. In less than a century, the learned and skilful teachers of the sciences became so common that, when any person or society offered a very small salary to hire one able professor, many presented themselves begging for the employment.

So it was in every other business, art, or profession. In all of them the numbers of the skilful multiplied to such an extent that there were usually more of them than needed. Hence, none but the skilful could get employment. Every one was compelled to qualify himself to do some kind of work, however humble and simple, with expertness. However diffi-

cult or fine his work, his pay was miserable. When
he could not attain skill in one avocation, he was
tacitly expelled and forced to seek another less
difficult or better adapted to his nature. If he failed
in all to equal or nearly equal the best, he was
reduced to pauperism and quasi-starvation.

To a certain extent, a like selection of skill took
place in the Eden of Labor; but it was in a peculiar
manner. It was organized and managed intelligently,
not left to the irregular and distressing operation of
the blind force of circumstances, or to the depressing
power of a few usurpers of the exclusive ownership
of the blessings God intended for all in the creation
of Nature.

To adjust the (1) accessions of QUANTITY, and (2)
superiorities of QUALITY, produced by *skill*, to the
rule of labor-time price, the Supreme Patriarch, in
his Economic Code, made several wise dispositions
conformed to the fundamental principle of the Reductional Theory.

Besides other classifications which I will explain
anon, he established a distinction of things and
occupations into, (1) NECESSARY, (2) COMMODIOUS, (3)
EXTRAVAGANT, and (4) PERNICIOUS. It was required
that every industry and product of industry be
classed under one of these designations or categories.
The policy of the State favored the necessary, protected the convenient, permitted the extravagant, and
prohibited the pernicious.

I do not wish to be understood to say that it is
possible to place each of the great number of things
composing the world's wealth or the industries producing them *absolutely* under one of these heads, by
direct recognition. These terms, necessary, commodious, extravagant, and pernicious, are often merely
comparative. A thing or business may belong to
one or the other of these classes according to circumstances. What is necessary may also be commodious. What is commodious may be also extravagant, or sumptuous. What is sumptuous or luxu-

7

rious may be also pernicious. Most things, however, have one of these four qualities more prominently marked, and should be classed according to the preponderance of one or the other of them; *but there is an ecomomic test* which is clear and practical, and it is precisely in an economic point of view that we have to consider the matter. Thus, in deciding whether a thing should be regarded as assignable to one or the other of these classes ITS PRICE in relation to the price of other articles of the same use is the important element for deciding whether it should be classed as necessary, merely commodious, or extravagant—unless by its intrinsic character it must be one of these, or even pernicious. Water is a necessary thing whatever may be the cost of procuring it, but let us look at things the classification of which, under these heads, depends upon their price. An example will explain this test better than an abstract statement of principle. For instance, a cup is a necessary article. If it be of crockery or tin, the cheapest and commonest that can be had, it cannot be classed otherwise than among necessary things. It is either that or nothing. If, by additional labor, better material, and superior art, the form and durability of an article be improved without greatly enhancing its cost, while however the common and cheaper kind is available, then the improved article ought to be classed among commodious things. But you may object and say: if the cup were made of glass it would be beautiful, while possessing all the qualities of utility and convenience. Now, under what head should I place a glass goblet, considering its utility, its convenience, and its beauty? If we were merely propounding a question of taste, merely deciding upon appearances, then of course we would assign the glass goblet to the sumptuous class; but we are solving a question of political economy—a question of rivalry between bare usefulness and beauteous usefulness by the test of their respective labor cost. Nothing is more beautiful and sumptuous, in an

artistic point of view, than glass ; but if the beautiful glass goblet is the easiest obtained, costs the same
or about the same as crockery or tin, and is equally
durable, it should be classed with necessary things.
If, however, all things considered, it is considerably
or even markedly more costly and there be cheaper
articles substantially as good, then I class the glass
goblet among merely convenient or commodious
things.   Now suppose a crystal goblet were artis-
tically carved at an expense much in excess of the
price of the (1) necessary or (2) commodious article.
In this case, it would be (3) sumptuous or extravagant.   Adorn it with gold and jewels so as to mar
its utility, convert it into a mere ornament, too fine
to be used, and waste much money in producing the
vain though beautiful thing, then it ought to be
regarded as (4) pernicious—a mere exhibition of the
vanity of its owner, combined with loss of utility,
and unproductive consumption of an inordinate
excess of labor-time.

This example of a cup or goblet regarded first as
necessary, next as commodious, then as extravagant
or sumptuous, and finally as pernicious, is sufficient
to give an adequate idea of the economic demarcation of the distinctions mentioned.   Other palpable
examples will doubtless suggest themselves to the
reader.   The general rule may now be stated.   The
commonest and cheapest, or only available thing
answering an indispensable want is (1) necessary
wealth ; but when the cost of making notably exceeds
that by which the want may be otherwise sufficiently
supplied, the thing is (2) commodious wealth ; when
for the sake of beauty, fineness, savor, or any other
artistic motive, a cost is incurred largely disproportionate to utility, the product is (3) extravagant or
sumptuous ; and when there is vain waste and no
utility, or any use contrary to good morals or health,
the thing and the work producing it are (4) pernicious.
It is manifest that when, by new inventions of labor-
saving and prolific machinery, things previously

sumptuous could be made so cheap as to be within the means of a commoner, they would then be reduced to the class of commodious or even of necessary articles.

If the process stopped here these distinctions would have been merely speculative, and of little practical use, but in the Eden of Labor they reduced the abstract principle to mathematical formulas applicable to all possible instances. By careful observation and exact analysis, they ascertained the proportions of cost in labor-time that would truly determine to which of these four categories any product belonged. Taking in each kind of thing, the cost of the necessary one, the commonest and cheapest but substantial article, *as a basis*, they devised a series of proportions of extra cost according to which articles of the same kind and use were to be regarded as necessary, commodious, extravagant, or pernicious. I pass over the manifold uses of this classification in the improvement of morals, the happiness of society, and good legislation, to attend only to its application in assessing THE REWARD OF SKILL.

CHAPTER V.

WE have already seen how the average labor-time
was ascertained and assessed for each kind and phase
of service or production, and this average was made
the exchangeable value of each thing. In assessing
the average value in cases where skill had an important effect, several points had to be considered.
(1) The skill used might only result in producing a
quantity of a product greater than the average, without a material difference of quality. In this event
no estimate above the average was made in favor of
skill; for it derived its just reward directly from the
greater quantity placed to its credit at the average price.
(2) The skill used might produce the average or nearly
the average quantity, but a better quality of work-
manship. In this case an estimate of the *extra* labor-
time an *average* workman would find it necessary to
consume in producing an equally well-executed piece
was made, and this estimate was added as part of the
average labor-time allowed the man of skill. The
products thus valued belonged of right, at the lowest,
to the commodious category. (3) But sometimes the
skilful workmen would produce a quantity *less* than
the average. In this case also, he would enjoy the
advantage of the last preceding rule which might
make him even, or give him more than the average
per measure of product. Here again the classification would be, at least, with commodious things. (4)
Yet, still more ambitious to produce something beautiful or otherwise excellent, and indeed sumptuous,
the workman might devote to it an inordinate proportion of labor-time. In this case the rule of extra

7*

labor-time would not apply; but the master-piece would be classed among sumptuous things, and its full cost in labor-time be assessed as its value. (5) Then there was the case of the *inventor* of some labor-saving machine, tool. or implement. In his favor the law allowed for a limited number of years the right to demand from those who used his invention a royalty calculated from time to time, not by his own conceit and greed of gain, but by the expert of the National Patent Office, and this not with design to enrich him, but to afford him ample indemnity for the labor-time, cost of experiments, and study-time used in perfecting his invention, and secure him leisure to exercise his genius in other improvements.

The works of skill, it is seen, were assigned according to circumstances, sometimes in one category, sometimes in another. Thus they would be subject to a general rule, which it is now the proper time to state, and to which the attention of the reader is called.

The assessed labor-time exchangeable value of products classed as (1) necessary and (2) commodious, was immediately paid for by credit on the books, or by cash in the national labor notes on making the delivery or consignment to the public proxy; but products classed as, (3) sumptuous were *not* paid for or credited till an actual purchaser was found.

The reason of the exception in this rule is manifest. The consumption of sumptuous things is not in the regular course of economic business, is not within the means of those whose earnings are limited to average labor-time value; it depends upon the caprice of taste or fancy, and not upon a common want. In a country like the Eden of Labor, where, from the nature of the organic plan, all enjoyed abundance, but none were disproportionately rich, sumptuous productions were beyond the reach of individuals; and only societies, communities, or congregations could purchase them to adorn their public edifices, squares, churches, galleries, monuments, and museums.

A question may have suggested itself : What legislation or custom did the founder of the Eden of Labor ordain or advise, with respect to workmen whose services or products, *by the fault of their unskilfulness*, were of a quality or quantity positively inferior to the average? The answer flows from the principles already stated. Of course such laborers suffered the loss caused by their own unskilfulness; first, the loss from deficiency in quantity; second, a *pro rata* discount carefully calculated by reversing the rule applied to ameliorations accomplished by skill. Besides, as in the case of sumptuous things, the low-graded product was not paid for till actually purchased from the proxy. Moreover, the waste of time and materials by unskilful workmen was otherwise discouraged. They were admonished, not only by their own losses and the danger of no sale, but by authority, that they must exert themselves to acquire the skill they lacked, or be more careful to exercise that skill if they possessed it. If they could not or would not do this, their defective goods or services were ruled out of the market, and they were thus forced to resort to some other industry in which they could labor in a workmanlike manner.

The yearly statistics, already explained, gathered and published at the general expense, enabled every one to know which pursuits were too numerously supplied with workmen, and which were deficient in the adequate number. With exact knowledge of what was wanted one might change to an employment better suited to his taste and talent; and as in each service the best qualified hands were preferred and favored, the result of every transfer thus induced was naturally that each particular trade or subdivision of work was carried on by only the most competent; or, at least, only by those who could work up to the average. As the reward of labor was always the same, in whatever division it was done,

it made no *pecuniary* difference to any one whether
he worked at one trade or another. No one had an
interest in there being an excessive number seeking
employment in any specialty. Hence, the equilibra-
tion of the labor demand and supply was easy . . .
spontaneously and with foreknowledge, the equation
preceded work and production, instead of following
disasters consequent upon necessitous or reckless
competition, and oppressive or ravenous monopoly.
There could be no cause or motive for strikes or
lock-outs under the reductional system.

A remarkable result of the reduction of all things
and services to real labor-time value was, the impossibility of *commercial* adventures or *credit* speculations
for the sake of enriching profit; and consequently
also *usury* in all its forms and disguises. Since no
man could ever get any pay or price for anything or
service, beyond the average labor-time measure, it is
clear he could never have a surplus capital greatly
exceeding that of any other able-bodied or skilful
workman. No one ever gets rich by his *own* labor
or *skill* only. The exceptional and considerable personal fortunes which were seen in the land of Nod,
and which were made by managing to get hold of
products under some deceptive and inequitable pretext or custom, were precluded. No one could inequitably appropriate a share or dividend of the
labor of others, no one could wrongfully obtain an
exclusive individual title to natural things. If such
appropriation is prevented, and every one is limited
to what can be counted as done only by his individual
effort, if every helper in the making of any product
took his exact proportion measured by labor-time,
it is clear individuals would respectively have no
plethoric capital to lend or invest; none would ever
have so much that its loan for usury would enrich
them. Indeed, since every body in the Eden of Labor
was under the common law of the averaged labor-
time standard, there was, as I have previously remarked, no margin for profit; and therefore it was

vain to think of lending or borrowing for any such selfish purpose. There was no occasion for CREDIT except that of brotherly kindness—neighborly assistance—the lending with hope for nothing thereby—so expressly urged in the counsel which God has given. (Luke vi. 34.)

Nevertheless, and by virtue of this very impotence of private capital as an instrument of private enrichment, there was plenty for common undertakings, public improvements, industrial co-operation and help of the neighbor.

An effect of the rapid increase of population from the beginning of the Adamic Patriarchate, was that a father's house and farm did not long remain large enough for all his sons, with their wives and children. In due course, it became necessary for these to go forth into a separate habitation . . . cultivate another field, or carry on another factory. During a first period, when this occasion arose, the father, his kin, and his neighbors—in fact the whole reduction or clan who were numerically hundreds, went to work, gathered and prepared materials, erected a dwelling, with usual out-buildings for each new family. At the same time they cleared the necessary ground for a single or co-operative field, or made and put up the necessary workshops or factories for single or combined labor as the case might be. All this they give to their young relations to start them in a new industrial career. Every helper in this work had been similarly helped before, and only returned to the young a benefit he had received from the old; and every one receiving such help contracted the obligation of returning it to a number as great as those who had helped him. The number of helpers or contributors, in each instance was so considerable that it was a small affair for each one, and the work was accomplished in a few days. It was a sort of frolic; and was always concluded by a grand celebration and feast. We have seen this beautiful custom revived in the "log-rollings" of the pioneers of America. At the opening of this country, whenever a new settler arrived, the hardy frontiersmen spontaneously assembled in force, and joyously co-operated in building a home for the stranger on any wild land he chose to take.

After a time, however, the supreme patriarch, considering certain inconveniences and derangements inherent to this method, substituted a more orderly and efficient one. By an equal assessment made during a few years on every man's earnings, a "Building and Improvement Fund" was raised and set apart. This was used to accomplish the same results as had been realized by the custom I have described. Those for whom it was so used were bound to repay in small yearly or quarterly instalments, and they did so, either in due course or by compulsion, so that after a while, the funds was constantly replenished by restitutions, and the tax was ratably diminished till it was reduced to almost *nil*, the repayments being sufficient for all the purposes of developing the industry of the country. When we consider that in the land of Nod (where individuals appropriated the labor of others and acquired full ownership of natural wealth), the capitalist made his undertakings or property repay the principal or keep it constantly renewed, besides deriving rent, interest, or profit sufficient for his opulent support, his luxurious pleasure, and even for a constant increase of the sum of his personal wealth, we see that to enrich others, wagemen and tenants, in the course of their life, actually paid for the machinery they wielded, and for the homes they rented, without ever becoming owners themselves. How much easier was it then for the producers of the Eden of Labor, where there was no usury, rental, or gain, no man allowed to levy a tribute from the labor of another, to pay his share of restitution to the fund that provided him with machinery to work with and a home to live in.

The operation of this system afforded every facility for the application of the exigences and principles of the DIVISION OF LABOR. In founding new farms and factories, the analysis of every detail of labor enabled the elders of a reduction or clan to determine their capacity, their mechanical appliances, and the number of each class of hands they should employ, so as to adjust each specialty of skill and the necessary machines in such proportions as fully to employ each other, leave no hiatus compelling one set of workmen or machines to wait on another, and, indeed, operate as a whole, so that no part should be idle or overdriven, but all be continuously and harmoniously engaged. While the Reductionese had each his own separate home, they gladly co-operated externally to secure the benefits of the developments of skill, the economy and increase, a proper division of labor is known to realize.

The Eden of Labor carried on COMMERCE with foreign countries. It may be asked, how could its reductionism (which was so rigorously adhered to in domestic exchanges) be adapted to trade with nations that allowed competition, usury, monopoly, and extortion of arbitrary exchange value for natural things, to have full sway? The mention of some of the incidents of trade with the land of Nod will answer this question. The currency of Nod was what we now-a-days call "hard money," silver and gold, which had become (from many causes too numerous to mention here) the circulating medium of that country. The currency of the reductions was the labor note I have described and the purchasing power of which I have explained. Yet, the reductions were in a land producing gold (Gen. ii 12), but the Reductionese never estimated gold otherwise than by the exact labor-time devoted to its extraction and its conversion into utensils and ornaments. On the other hand, the Nodlanders sought eagerly for the metal, and readily gave for it values far greater than its own. For instance, they would give a ton of fine flour for an ounce of gold dust, though it took no more work to gather an ounce of gold than to produce an ounce

of flour. At the same time, if they offered gold for
flour, oil, wool, iron, or any other product, the Reductionese would not give more than the measure of
labor-time embodied in the wool or iron for a weight
of gold produced by the same amount of labor-time.
The same happened whenever the Nodlanders offered
anything they regarded as extra valuable on account
of its rarity, beauty, fineness, or flavor. Since they
adjusted values by demand and supply, or the exigencies of monopoly, they could not use their coin
and costly luxuries in trading with the Reductionese,
while the latter disposed of their own gold and other
products which the Nodlanders esteemed, for great
comparative quantities of necessary and substantial
things, such as cloth, coal, iron, tools, cutlery, or
glass.

The reader now, of course, sees plainly enough
that the labor-time standard of exchange, and the
reductional labor-note, by their necessary operation,
presented insuperable impediments to the production
and sale of COSTLY LUXURIES intended for private
consumption. With his real, personal earnings, by
the equal labor measure, no man could acquire the
means of indulging frequently in extravagant and
vanitous articles or revelry. For instance, a man
who earned only three hundred days of equal labor-
time per annum, as every one did in the Eden of
Labor, and who had to pay by the same measure of
value for his clothing, shelter, food, and so forth,
could not often have the means of paying for anything into which one or more years of labor-time had
been absorbed, such as a piece of blonde lace, a mosaic
table, a panel of Goblins tapestry, or a set of Sevres
porcelain.

On the other hand, most of the labor-time which,
in the land of Nod, was wasted on sumptuousness
and every other costly pleasure, was saved in the
Eden of Labor for better purposes. The Reductionese
necessarily refrained from making the excessively
fine, dearly ornamented, and tempting but pernicious

things consumed only by inordinately rich people—
for there was no such class of men in the country.
Nearly all the population were employed in helping
to produce the *substantial and beautiful*, BUT CHEAP,
things consumed by commoners generally. This
caused an enormous difference between the popular
wealth and well-being of the Eden of Labor and the
land of Nod. In the latter, millions of men were
kept at hard work manufacturing silks, equipages,
tapestries, plate, laces, artificial flowers, sculptures,
and other luxuries destined for the private enjoyment
of the rich, and which the rich only could afford.
Besides this, hundreds of thousands were engaged
in pernicious works — manufacturing intoxicating
liquors, raising and preparing tobacco, making cards
and dice, and keeping gambling hells, and pursuing
many other avocations of even greater infamy. Then,
with these, there was a large proportion driven to
idle pauperism by the monopolizing system itself.
On the other hand, under the rule of Reductionism,
every man worked for what was useful and pleasurable, and *available to all*, but not for anything pernicious.

The grand consequence of this direction of all labor
to that which was good for the masses—this immense
turning of labor from costly and pernicious to necessary and commodious products and service, was
ABUNDANCE of all commodities and pleasures that
were honestly desirable. The whole people lived in
comfort; nay, more, they enjoyed an overflow of
temporal blessings, a great plenty of the best fruits
of the earth and of the good things fabricated by
skilful hands and ingenious machinery.

The inhabitants of this land of equity and brotherhood, by their diligence and thrift, brought forth and
enjoyed excellent and ample shelter, food, raiment,
fuel, tools, and intellectual objects. Their country
was thickly dotted with fair and substantial dwellings—also warehouses, factories, and mills—temples,
and other public edifices—farms, mines, and wooded

8

mountains, towns and villages, roads and canals. They had profusion of grain and fruit, oil and vegetables, fish and flesh, cattle and poultry, milk, eggs, and honey. They made as much as each and all could consume of durable and beautiful stuffs for clothing—woollens, cottons, linens, silks, shoes, and hats, in every needed variety within the means of labor-time fortunes. They supplied themselves with wood and coal without stint. They possessed all manner of ingenious tools, implements, and machinery—also vessels, vehicles, and beasts of burden, for saving labor and doing perfect work designed for general advantage, at labor-time prices. Their homes were made more comfortable and agreeable by every convenient and neat article of furniture and ornament—carpets, bedding, and curtains—utensils and plate—well-provided pantries, larders, and kitchens. Finally, they had full measure of private libraries and studios, public museums and galleries, stored with good books, paintings, sculptures, musical instruments, specimens, models, and other results of science, fine art, and literature; and, besides this, they all, without exception, had leisure to derive the real benefits and pure pleasures such things afford.

Be it, however, noted here, this immense and delightful prosperity was on one condition: "Seek ye first the kingdom of God and His righteousness; and all these things will be added unto you." (Matt. vi. 33; Luke xii. 31.)

Be it also noted that so long as they fulfilled this condition *no* set or clique among them had or could have those invidious and disproportionate vanities, enjoyments, fineries, delicacies, equipages, adornments, and other sumptuosities which a favored and distinct few, in other countries, under the sanction of uncharitable institutions and laws, succeed in drawing to their selfish selves alone.

Another consequence of Reductionism was the PROGRESS OF THE ARTS entirely *towards this inexpensive production:* not to things and enjoyments which only exorbitant and inequitable fortunes could compass; but those that the full and honest portion of labor could properly acquire. As costly luxuries were precluded, cheap ones were invented or discovered. What was accomplished in this line by true science and ingenuity was wonderful. Objects uniting beauty and utility—amusements and recreations displaying admirable æsthetical taste were brought within the reach of every person. Govern ment assisted this tendency to the combination of artistic excellence and adornment with economy and cheapness. Experiments were made at public expense. Associations contributed to them. Thus ways were opened by which works previously too costly to be advantageously undertaken were made to gratify the tastes of laborers who earned only, but fully, their just compensation. The course of industry and genius was always and intentionally pointed in the direction of the best place, the best workers, the best kind, the greatest quantity, and the least cost in labor-time. Works of art were copied and multiplied by tens of thousands, and executed with constant approaches to perfection; but I have no space for details of the admirable results.

The one condition of average labor-time being strictly complied with, it was all the better that labor-saving machinery was invented—that any number of new commodities were produced, that population increased—because such progress and multiplication were of equal benefit to every person—an immediate and direct gain and blessing to all. There were more luxuries and more rest for every individual.

A last result remains to be stated before I close this chapter. The concert of so many hands and of all machinery, the co-operation of the entire population—men, women, and children, and of every force or device that could make labor most prolific—to the grand and sole purpose of evolving only such wealth and consumable values as every industrious man

could afford to procure, resulted in the making of
such extraordinary quantities of this character and
kind, that it was soon perceived a great REDUC-
TION OF THE LENGTH OF A LAWFUL DAY'S LABOR
was not only possible but necessary. As every man
had to eat his bread by the sweat of his face, and as
by every one of them doing six hours' work per day
a great excess was brought forth of whatsoever could
satisfy the reasonable wants and gratify the equitable
desires of every member of society, the Supreme
Patriarch from time to time issued his proclamation
reducing the lawful day's labor first to five and then
to four hours. This was the inherent effect of the
system.   While art continually brought new luxuries within the reach of all at very insignificant cost,
it so multiplied production of this nature, that it exceeded consumption, so that the people could produce
in four hours not only as much as they did before in
six hours, but also within that time all the other
commodities they had recently succeeded in cheaply
producing. At the same time, as there was no inducement or market for work or articles absorbing long
measures of labor-time, it followed inevitably that
the labor of producing the maximum of all necessaries, comforts, and luxuries, must be equally divided
among those who were to have their portion of this
production. Since there was abundance for all by
five hours' work instead of six, and since there were
no monopolists of natural things to force the masses
to competition and pauperism, since there were none
interested to compel others by starvation to enter the
miserable service of vanity and excesses, the effect
was that the Reductionese, to a man, gladly assented
to—nay, hailed as a triumph, the diminution of their
respective toil as a blessing. It deprived no one of
anything, but added to rest, recreation, and leisure
to acquire knowledge—contemplate and study the
Divinity in His works, and worship His glory and
beneficence. It was easy in each instance to find the
proper quantum of the diminution, since all produc-

tion was measured by its labor-time, the aggregate of the excess of production over consumption, gave, in the proportion of population to a day's labor-time, the exact number of hours or minutes of the necessary diminution. How different in effect is this system from that which brings about strikes and lock-outs, accompanied by the destitution and ruin we hear of now-a-days. Need I say how happy a people were who had so much leisure to improve their minds, make progress in true science and beneficent art, and who were free to enjoy their Sabbaths in rest and peace?

In future chapters I will give account of many details, I have omitted in this preliminary sketch; and shall tell the history of the corrupt and iniquitous institutions of the land of Nod, the conquest and enslavement of the Eden of Labor by the Nodlanders; and trace the causes of the universal sinfulness that provoked the anger of God to inflict the all-destroying Deluge.

Formula of the Reductionese Currency.

THE EDEN OF LABOR

commands the Public Proxy of the Reduction of Havilah to deliver to bearer, on demand, products of industry of the value of

FIVE HOURS

average labor time, according to the Tariff of prices current at the date hereof.

Havilah, 72d of Fifth Month, A. M. 450.

Accepted by
ZEBADIAH, pub. proxy.

IDDO JOEZER,
Accountant.

8*

CHAPTER VI.

PERSONAL SERVICE AND ITS REWARD.

But, before I pass on, I should revert to a particular element or feature of the economic system of the Eden of Labor, which, to avoid complexity, I have merely mentioned incidentally, and the special characteristics of which I left to implication. It is the principle which should determine the compensation due to such personal services as were *not* embodied, by weight and measure, in products of industry.

The services, for example, of domestic servants or of scientific and artistic educators essentially contribute to the making of products; but they do not *tangibly* take part in manufacturing or constituting the material form of those products. Such services are collateral or remote; but nevertheless they are positive.

This is a matter of primary importance; for it is necessarily a factor in the labor-time value of products. Immediately after the expulsion, Adam, with hopeful Eve by his side, applied himself to cultivating the brier-grown and rebellious soil. While, with loose stones and boughs, he constructed a temporary hut—while he built the first little furnace, extracted and smelted the small quantity of ore, inter-hammered and hardened the few pounds of iron which he needed to make the first knife, axe, hatchet, draw-knife, adze, saw, pot, needle, and nails—while he went on to fashion the first spade and plough, rake and hoe—while he cleared, dug, and ploughed a few acres of ground, and planted corn and vegetables, and while he was also occasionally slaughtering and flaying a lamb, Eve was occupied in watching and herding the few sheep they possessed, cooking

the food, currying and softening the skins, sewing
the skins together for raiment, bringing water in a
large gourd from the spring, cleaning the house,
making up the bed, and mending the clothes. Need
I mention the solicitude and care of these two for
each other's comfort and health—the melodious
hymns of praise they sang while they beat musical
measure on their sweet-sounding cymbals—their conversation in which they rehearsed the moral and religious lessons they had learned from the angels, and
thus renewed the life of their souls? What I wish
the reader to note is, that a portion of the work they
each performed was not directly embodied *in* the
commodities of objects they produced.

Observe that when one of them was, during sickness, nursed by the other—when Eve swept the
house, when Adam defended her against wild beasts
—the time and effort were not even transiently deposited in any intermediate object wherein its quantita-
tive *product* might have been weighed or measured,
but was absorbed directly by the metaphysical as
well as physical person to whom the service was
rendered.

Observe also that when their respective labor could
be measured objectively in a product made for consumption, there was always a part due to the collateral
service of the other, though not quantitatively and
manually embodied therein. True, Adam's hand
alone cultivated and gathered the yearly crop of
corn; but he calculated that it was several times
larger than it would have been had he been obliged
to interrupt the cultivation to prepare his food, and
to do the other desultory and lighter work performed
by Eve. True, Eve's hand alone picked wild fruit
from the neighboring trees or carried water from the
spring, but in this and in every other respect she felt
that she was unable to make sufficient provision for
herself, and that she was able to give the necessary
time to her special avocations, because Adam's time

was fully and uninterruptedly devoted to his appropriate functions.

Observe, moreover, that the final cause, the last term, the *focus* of all their labor, in every particular, whether direct, collateral, or through commodities, was the physical and spiritual sustenance, development, and renewal of *themselves*. They mutually furnished products and rendered services to this end; and all the labor-time expended by one on or for the other was returned by that other. It was reabsorbed by the person from whence it came; and there fulfilled the ultimate purpose for which it was originally put forth.

Therefore, they were mutual *helpers;* and each was entitled to a share of labor-time represented, if not specially embodied, in the manual products made by the other.

By and by children were born unto them, and a series of new conditions in the economy of society presented themselves. The conditions were: firstly, the necessity of providing, with all kinds of subsistence, helpless persons who could make no immediate return—give nothing in exchange for what they received; and, secondly, the necessity of expending labor-time in education—that is to say, in sowing and cultivating knowledge and virtue in the minds of their children.

Thus, then, a new function or work was added to the many Adam and Eve were already performing; but, far from being irksome to them, it was their greatest delight. Before the birth of a child the spouses were doubly one. Now they were triply one. Previous to having children they were themselves the focus, the objective aim of every labor they performed; and now, with children, the self-object was not changed; for it was only enlarged. They regarded the children as parts or members of themselves. Their offspring were, as popular parlance expresses it to this day, their own flesh and blood.

As the children grew up, the unerring foresight of Adam saw what was necessary to prepare them for *society;* and for that inevitable consequence of social membership, the Division of Labor. Hence, he diligently taught them the divine precepts—impressed them with his faith—exhorted them to religious obedience—and trained each of them to excel in a distinct branch of industry.

As soon as Cain could pull up a weed, his father took him into the field and gave him practical instruction in every phase and operation of agriculture, till he became an adept. As soon as Abel could run as fast as a lamb, his mother brought him with her to help in shepherding the flock, and taught him all the means of controlling them—also how to shear, slaughter, and flay them—preserve or tan their skins. In due time he attained a complete proficiency. The same course was pursued with every son and daughter. Each was brought up and trained in a special department of labor; so that, when they were grown, the work formerly performed by the father alone for all the once helpless members of the family, was now divided among them, according to their functions and the specialties of their skill. The family was, nevertheless, the same *unit;* and provided for itself *as a unit*, by a multitude of hands and a variety of labor all working in harmony to accomplish a common purpose.

This was the primary stage of society. With it the polytechnic labors of Adam ceased, and the era of the division of labor commenced. By a necessary evolution, or the force of circumstances, Adam's time was now consumed in the performance of his duties as instructor, lawgiver, priest, and director of the numerous community his family now formed.

His duties became more and more arduous as population and specializations of labor became more and more numerous. It was at last requisite that he should appoint subordinate assistants, a hierarchy of help, and government was organized.

His sons with their children went out from the original trunk, as branches from a tree or vine. They formed new and plainly distinguishable families; but their dependence on the original stem, or rather on the whole body, continued to be, for a long time, directly manifest. Each family was engaged in a particular work which produced only one or a few things proper for its existence. Their works or products, regarded severally and without exchange would have been fragmentary, inconsequent, and inadequate; but, regarded in their seriation, it was plainly apparent that they formed a well-arranged and well-manœuvred industrial army. It was still distinctly manifest that individuals, however different their persons and occupations, were only parts of one organic body. This their great father assiduously pointed out to them. He took every occasion to teach them, in various forms of words, the truth which was afterwards lost and remained in oblivion for ages, but which our Lord Jesus Christ revived and reordained, that they were one body having many members, and that though the members had different offices they were all members of one another, economically as well as spiritually, that though, or rather because each, a different individuality and ability, rendered a different service, or furnished a different product, it was itself essential to the whole, helpless by itself, suffered from the sufferings of each of the others, and communicated its own pains to all the rest.

When population had increased to tens and hundreds of millions, and mankind had formed itself into apparently disconnected communities, tribes, and nations, and when in the great complication, division and subdivision of specialities, there was danger that workmen, traders, and professors might more easily lose sight of the all-comprising organic unity, the supreme patriarch would redouble his efforts to disseminate his principles, and imbue the people with their truth and importance.

I imagine one of his discourses might have been epitomized as follows:—

My children: When your mother and myself were sent out of Paradise, God left our persons in possession of two natures, one physical, the other metaphysical. The one consisted of bodily strength, the other of intellectual and moral will. These we applied to accomplish our labor; and the product of that labor we applied to the renovation of our physical and metaphysical person. We were two individuals, each having this dual nature, but the two individuals were naturally one person. By generation, this doubly dual person, dual in attribute and dual in body, was multiplied. By the birth of children, it became physically triple; and then by the formation of families, millions of similar triplicate units arose; but, in the same manner as we were one economically and morally, they all still constituted, with us, the same personal or corporate unit we were before they were born.

Labor was apportioned among you—divided into a great variety of operations, each of which was assigned to a person, group, company, or series of individuals; but this was really a marshalling and concert of particularized industry, to make it more efficient, and to augment the quantity as well as improve the quality of its fruits. The more labor was divided into separate and single operations, the greater was the mass of products from the sum total of effort; but the division was never designed to enable one person or occupation to appropriate more than its labor-time reward from the common and aggregate product. It was for the good of each and all. It was possible only by concert and co-operation, and its increase of fruit was justly divisible only in copartnership.

The cause of all labor is the production of things fit for the preservation, the renewal, the development of *life*. Man spends his strength, mind, and life in procuring things which he consumes in order to support, cultivate, and reproduce that same strength, mind, and life. They are himself; and hence his work is all for the continuous reproduction of himself—not of his animal body only, but his body and soul. In him—through the procurement (by physical and metaphysical effort) of food, clothing, fuel, shelter, science, and virtue, for himself—his labor *terminates*. This is the focus to which all the reflectors and rays of labor converge. No matter how complex the arrangement, the multiplicity and divisions of functions and tasks—no matter how disconnected from the production of something fit to sustain and replenish strength, mind, and life, the work of any individual may seem, it is really done for this purpose. The studies and researches of the philosopher, the machines of the inventor, the various and complex appliances of art, the administration of the laws, worship and obedience to God, the teachings and admonitions of religion, the organization of society itself, the gratification of the senses by comforts, luxuries, and pleasures, are auxiliaries to the great sum of material production of which every man must have a share in order that he may live and learn now and forever.

Whoever labors, labors for this; for, though he may misapply his strength and intellect, mistake evil for good, his design is always to attain what he thinks is good; and even the worst man, he who neglects spiritual, moral, and intellectual life to work only for material life, thinks his folly is wisdom, his selfishness justice—thinks he is really replenishing his rational and æsthetical nature. Under a wicked delusion, he mistakes aberration and declension for progress. If, on the contrary, a man rises above sordid materiality, and labors not only for the continuance of physical life, but also for that which is conducive to æsthetic and religious life, he does so with the same conviction that he is seeking the supreme good. He regards body and mind as interdependent—the vigor of one as participating in the vigor of the other. They are both himself, and he works for both as one, and as constituting that one person he knows as himself. It is by providing for both these natures that he perpetuates himself integrally in this world. If he neglects either, both are deteriorated. If he takes care of physical vigor only, his sensual comforts or pleasures may be multiplied for a time, but he gradually sinks into ignorance and vice, loses the science, industry, morality and religion which previously enabled him to devise and realize, in a prudent and constant manner, even material good—loses self-control, rushes into absurdity and abuse, is disappointed, curses God, and dies.

Let it not, therefore, be imagined that the reductional system discourages or proposes to hinder the cultivation of the fine arts, the demands of man for recreation and amusement, the progress of true science. On the contrary, it embraces the true and beautiful as equal in importance to the good, THE COMMODIOUS AND SUMPTUOUS, when procured without inequitable appropriation, as legitimately desirable as that which is absolutely NECESSARY. Hence we have in the Eden of Labor great numbers engaged in occupations, works, and professions of almost every kind carried on in Nodland. Only those that extort usury, profit, or rent beyond labor-time service, do not exist in this country; for they are impossible under our economic system; but we have all the wonderfully manifold and complex specializations of trades and avocations proper in a country where virtue reigns supreme, and where the highest and finest aspirations of human nature are promoted. We neglect no art or means of enlarging, multiplying, and facilitating the happiness of mankind. It would be too minute and lengthy to mention all the specialties which economy, taste, and genius have invented or induced; but we may define the classes into which they are divided by the principles of the Reductional System.

Besides other views, labor may be examined under

9

three aspects, and these aspects may be considered distinctively or together. We may study labor with special regard to (1) the Laborer, or (2) the Product, or (3) the Final Cause. We may study all three simultaneously as indivisible. This combined view enables us to make the following classification or division of the whole matter:—

1. There are labors applied to the production of tangible articles and commodities intended *for immediate sale and consumption*. On the completion and delivery of the product, the workman, in this case, immediately receives his reward, in average labor-time currency, from the purchaser, who, by consuming the product, is preserved and invigorated. *Ex. gr.*, a farmer produces some vegetable, and sells it to a mechanic, who eats it, and is thereby nourished.

2. There are labors applied to the production of things not only tangible, but durable or permanent; such as furniture, buildings, etc., not intended for immediate or rapid consumption, but which the laborer makes and delivers *new* to others for their use or enjoyment in furtherance or revival of their material, æsthetical, or spiritual life, or of all of these three together. This case is that of a laborer making a new or original product, the consumption of which is to be gradual and slow. Such a product may be immediately appraised as a totality or entire thing, according to the labor time embodied in it; and be paid for as such in the same manner as a commodity made, sold, and delivered for immediate consumption. The *thing* here, as in the preceding case, presents in itself all the elements of its original value, and nothing else. Hence it belongs entirely to the makers, who may retain it as absolutely and wholly their own, until they are paid all the labor-time value it embodies.

3. But there are labors applied to *old* things, already paid for, and belonging to some single natural person who employs the laborer to repair them, or add something to them. *Ex. gr*, the laborer who

repairs buildings, mends tools, or washes and irons clothes belonging to another, who retains and continues to use and gradually consume them. In such a case it is hardly ever possible to estimate the reward due to the laborer by the proportionate or absolute increase of the value of the object on which the work has been done. Suppose, for instance, a carpenter goes over the leaky roof of an old house, puts in a shingle here and a shingle there, and makes the roof perfectly tight, it would be generally impracticable to measure his labor-time by examining the roof itself; and therefore the reward of his labor, for want of a better means of estimate, must be the *actual* labor-time devoted to the work, and be paid out of the owner's *proportional* share of the sum-total of products.

4. There are labors which are applied, like the preceding, to the maintenance and repair of old things, but with the difference that the things belong to and are being used by *several or many private or corporate owners*. *Ex. gr.*, laborers who repair theatres, club houses, churches, or other things belonging to societies, companies, etc. In this instance also, the reward must be according to the *actual* labor-time, without regard to the value of the thing on which the work is done, but with due regard to the laborer's title to a proportionate part of the owner's share in the sum total of production.

5. There are labors which are applied to the repair of *public things*, such things as it is the faculty and function of a community or government to provide and maintain. *Ex. gr*, the labor of those who repair public roads, bridges, sewers, court-houses, prisons, etc. Here again only the *actual* labor-time compared with the sum total production must be the measure of reward.

6. There is labor which is *directly* applied to the physical nature of some one person distinctly from every other person. *Ex. gr.*, the labor of a nurse, a barber, a doctor, etc.

7. There is labor which is *directly* applied to the pnysical invigoration of several persons at a time. *Ex. gr.*, hospital-nurses, house-keepers in orphanages, hotel servants, etc.

8. There is labor which is applied directly, in each instance, to the *metaphysical nature* of some *one* person distinctly from all other persons. *Ex. gr.*, the lesson of a private teacher of vocal or instrumental music, the private lesson of any artist or professor, etc.

9. There is labor which is applied *directly* to the invigoration and revival of the *metaphysical nature of several* or many persons at a time. *Ex. gr.*, the labor of school-masters, actors, lecturers, etc.

10. There is labor which is applied to the moral, æsthetical and intellectual nature of the body politic or *public order*. *Ex. gr.*, the labor of legislators, magistrates, etc.

For these categories, except the first and second, the rule of reward should be this: As the total number of all kinds of laborers is to the total number of collateral helpers, so is the total labor-time of all kinds of laborers to the total share of labor-time due to the collateral helpers out of the sum of products, which total share should be distributed *pro rata* among the individuals of the class, according to the actual labor-time of each.

Let me explain.

If you study these divisions you will see they may be reduced in several ways, so that the whole matter would be embraced in a less number of parts. In one view, labor is applied, (1) *through products*, to the ultimate purpose of all labor, the preservation and renewal of persons in both their physical and metaphysical natures, or (2) *without an intermediary*, to the same end. In another view labor is applied, (1) to make *new* things, (2) to repair *old* things, (3) to render direct help or service to persons physically, (4) to render direct help or service to persons metaphysically, that is to say, to directly address their rational, moral, æsthetical, or spiritual nature.

When labor is applied to things, the action passes through various and devious channels, is carried by different vehicles from one cross road to another, is transferred from one object or envelop to another, is transformed in various ways (the process or course being sometimes very complex and crooked), till, in the form of a product fit for human life, it is consumed by one person or many, and realizes its appropriate effect, the special efficiency of its nature and quality, whether beneficial or injurious in the body and soul of the consumer.

It often happens that labor is embodied in physical things specially designed to be mere vehicles or instruments of a metaphysical effect. Books, engravings, newspapers, wood-cuts, paintings, statuary, music-books, clocks, watches, jewelry, toys, artificial flowers, equipages, chess-men, cards, and other gaming utensils, ornaments of all kinds, theatres, school-houses, colleges, museums, conservatories, observatories, aquariums, scientific apparatus and collections, churches, the printer's type and presses, the sculptor's chisels, the painter's colors and brushes, the musician's instruments, the actor's or masquerader's disguise, the naturalist's specimens, the author's pen, all these, and many other physical things, are made for and consumed by the metaphysical nature of man. Nevertheless, since they are tangible, their æsthetical and rationalistic effect, whether for good or for evil, does not prevent them from being directly measured or estimated in labor-time currency. In this respect they are like commodities or media made specially for physical life. They present in a material form the specific data by which the appraiser may reckon the exact quantity of labor-time necessary to make them.

When labor is applied to *persons*, the action is, in many cases, simple and the transfer immediate—the help or service is absorbed physically or metaphysically, without the intervention of media, by a single person or many; and it strengthens or vivifies, weakens or perverts the two natures of the one or many by whom it is absorbed. These services require little or no intervention of commodities or instruments. They consist, as it were, in the direct consumption, by one man, of the strength and intellect of another. Such are the doctor's prescriptions, the lawyer's pleading, the school master or lecturer's instructions, the preacher's sermons, the nurse's care, the servant's daily housework, the washer and ironer's renovations, the actor's performance, the musician's concert, the watchman's rounds, the soldier's guard, the judge's trial of causes, the governor's administration, and many other labors and services which are not applied to or merged in a merchantable object—*not* conveyed in the substance and form of an appraisable thing, but are transferred immediately from person to person.

Those who, without producing a tangible object, disseminate knowledge and inculcate virtue, those who relieve the producer from desultory cares that would cause interruption and delay—those who minister to normal amusement and relaxation—those who take care of the toiler's person or the persons of his children, or protect his liberty and property, or restore and preserve his health — really *help* to make the commodities or articles the producer produces. They contribute to procure him the health, the strength, the willingness, the constancy, the intelligence, and the time necessary to the pursuit of his labors diligently, continuously, and advantageously. Though the *quantum* of assistance they contribute is not measurable and appreciable *in* the weight, volume, or elements of the commodities and other material objects, that quantum is really there. A part of the labor-time embodied, and counted for the ostensible maker or repairer, is due to the collateral helper. There is on every material product a claim which the collateral helpers may rightfully assert. The products must, therefore, pay back their labor, however indirect it may be. The helpers must have a quantum of the products or die. We know that education, discipline, practice, devotion to duty, confidence in social protection and justice, hope of equitable reward founded on the honesty of fellow creatures, are prerequisites and concomitants of material production, and have stamped their seal upon it; and, alas! we know also that these prerequisites and concomitants are not adduced or put forth spontaneously, but are the fruits of the labor-time of persons whose vocation it has been to impart them to individuals and society.

This, then, is the cycle of all labor. It is put forth by the bodies and souls—by the physical, intellectual, moral, and religious natures of the laborers—and sent through many intricate channels of circulation and process, exchange and distribution, help and co-operation, directly and collaterly, to be integrally reabsorbed by the laborers themselves. Thus new power to labor is created; and labor is again put forth to be again reabsorbed; and so on it moves, *ad infinitum*, in a circular series of evolutions. In this respect it obeys the law of the correlation of forces.

The physical and metaphysical natures of man are the colaborers and copartakers of the fruitful effort and return. The hand and the heart—the belly and members—the senses and mind—the flesh and spirit of all laborers, whatever special work each of them may do, are copartners; and each furnisher of these forces of body or soul, is entitled to a full, but not unequal, *restoration* of what he has expended in labor-time for others.

By consuming the production of one term of labor man is preserved and invigorated—acquires new strength and life, and is thereby enabled to accomplish another course of production. It is *he*, himself, properly speaking, who, as the final term of industry, is *re*produced; and not the things he cultivates or makes. The latter, in the economic scheme, are reproduced incidentally to the reproduction of the person of the laborer. While he works he is destroying previous products—his collateral and general assistants do so likewise; and from this destruction they derive the forces which enable them to carry on their work. When the product is made and finished—stands forth complete—it is only at a stage or term of its *transit*—it, itself, is not the final cause of its being made—it was so made only to be absorbed in man—it is still only a potentiality or possibility—and attains its end only when, by consumption, it has been, as it were, transmuted and transformed into the forces constituting human life. All the forces of production and reproduction, material and spiritual, principal and auxiliary, concentrate in the form, attributes, and nature of man.

Hence a man owes to others *all* he consumes of the labor of others—no less, no more. If he returns this he is entitled to acquittance. Till he does so, he is a debtor. If he takes, wastes, and does not restore, he is a defaulter. If he takes *increase* from him who makes full restoration in labor-time value—for example, exacts more than unit for unit, borrowed money for borrowed money—he takes more than his due—is guilty of usury; for his due is only the labor-time he has expended on others.

The assessment of the reward due to those whose labor is immediately embodied in merchantable things has been fully explained, and presents little or no difficulty; but the practicability of appraising and paying, (1) the repairs done on the not-to-be sold property of others, or of the public, (2) the collateral or direct help or service rendered by one person to the person of another, or to the social body, is not so obvious.

The political economists of Nodland, the sons of Cain, would answer the difficulty I suggest by the words capital, labor-fund, rent, profit, usury, and hire. Beginning at the final results of their iniquitous system, they would show the fact that there are classes of men who have the private ownership of, and derive income from, nearly all the money and property in the world—that the revenues of these fortunates are sufficient to pay wages to workmen who make repairs, wages to artists who minister to luxury, wages to servants and educators who refresh the body and mind ; and that still there is a surplus left for the appropriators of that surplus to make new investments and gather new remainders. They would show how a class appropriates all the benefits of the division of labor; and that the wage class, the real producers, repairers, helpers, co-operators, had nothing, no surplus, which they could call their own ; and hence need not trouble themselves about providing the cost of renovating property and mind, should not think of anything but performing their daily task of servitude.

But this answer is not possible in the Eden of Labor, where such lions cannot seize upon, and divide as they please, the fruit of the labor of others. In the Eden of Labor no one appropriates more than the fruits of his own labor-time, and his proper proportion of the benefits of the division of labor. For instance, no one appropriates all the benefits of a labor-saving machine, but all those who work with it are entitled to a justly appraised share of the increased product it enables them to make. If it is a spinning-wheel, a plough, or a sewing machine, worked by *one* for himself, he gets all the increased product it gives; but, if a mill or farm worked by many, they divide equitably the saving or increase it bestows. In the Eden of Labor no one can afford to pay wages; for no one can get more than what is due for his own *pro rata* of labor-time. Hence there can be no exceptional private accumulation of capital for building and repairs, no private appropriators to determine and distribute the pay of artists, educators, domestics, nurses, and other direct servitors of persons.

Hence the reductional system requires:—

1. That, as already explained in previous discourse, careful statistics should show the sum total

of absolute labor-time consumed by the ostensible maker, of all new products, and of labor-time left in old products put upon the market by their private owners for integral conversion into money.

2. That, on the other hand, careful statistics, embracing the whole people, should show the items and sum total of labor-time consumed, (1) in repairing paid products undergoing the process of personal or social consumption; and (2) in rendering direct personal service to persons, societies, or the State.

3. That in valuing every product put upon the market for integral conversion into money, the experts should, *firstly*, ascertain the absolute and ostensible labor-time embodied in them; *secondly*, should thereunto ADD a *pro rata* of the total labor-time of the repairers of things and helpers of persons.

4. That the price of each product put upon the market should represent both the ostensible average labor-time and a due proportion of the collateral labor-time of all classes of repairers of things, servitors of persons, and servitors of the body politic, so that, for example, if the ostensible labor-time of the maker of any one thing is five hours and the proportion of the collateral labor-time of repairers and servitors is three hours, then eight hours should be the market price of that thing.

5. That the share of the price accruing to the ostensible makers or owners should be credited to their individual accounts, respectively.

6. That the proportion accruing to collateral labor-time should be credited to a general fund; and that this should be apportioned according to the statistics among the Reductions, Clandoms, Tribedoms, Kindoms, and Patriarchdoms, to be distributed to the repairers of things, servitors of persons and servitors of the body politic, respectively and individually, according to the actual labor-time of the service of each of them.

7. That, besides this, the Reduction, Clandom, Tribedom, Kindom, or Patriarchdom, in order to pay

for the labor of *new* works needed for the common
use or body politic, should have a TAX FUND levied
proportionally on the sums credited to the accounts
of both categories, viz., of ostensible producers and
collateral producers, according to the labor-time
credited to each person.

8. That a Patriarchdom, Kindom, Tribedom, Clandom, or Reduction should pay for things furnished
it, or repairs done for it, or personal service rendered
it, by warrants drawn on its general fund or its special tax fund, according to the actual labor-time it
consumes, thereby enabling its furnishers or servitors to obtain their proper *pro rata* of the sum total
of products, at the average labor time price of any
particular product they may choose to take.

9. That the share or amount of the personal service of others, which each individual is entitled to
have and consume, during a year, should be determined, in labor-time, according to the statistical data,
so that he cannot appropriate more than his proportion, but if he consumes less he may profit by his
economy.

10. That the same rules of apportionment, consumption, and economy should apply to corporate
establishments and co-operative companies: they being
treated in their dealings with the market or body
politic as individuals, but bound to do strict justice,
and pay proportionate compensation to their members
respectively.

11. That the average number of calls or cases of a
lawyer, doctor, or other one whose service is rendered
to private persons individually, should be ascertained
by statistics; and each distinct individual or corporation who receives the benefit of a call or attention to
a particular case, should on his certificate be charged
with its appropriate labor-time, and that time be
credited to the servitor.

12. That individual or single servitors of persons
making no tangible market products, viz., a professor
of any science or art, a school-master, a lecturer, or

the like, serving several or many persons *simultane-ously*, should be credited their actual labor-time on the books of their reduction, and that time be charged *pro rata* to those who avail themselves of the common service; for example, each of the simultaneous par-takers should procure tickets from the public proxy, or from a deputy proxy detailed for that purpose, and each taker of a ticket should be charged with his *pro rata* of the whole actual labor-time credited to the servitor. Hence, if a school-master devotes one hour to teaching the children of twenty-five parents; he would be credited with that hour, and each parent be charged with one twenty-fifth of an hour, or four "strives" of work in average labor-time currency.

13. That the rule last stated should apply to the benefit of repairers of things, or servitors of persons working together, not as corporators, but tempora-rily, such as a company of actors, a band of musicians, a squad of scavengers doing their work or service for several or many persons simultaneously. In such a case, each member of the company, band, or squad should be credited with the actual labor time of his service, and the takers of checks for that service should be charged respectively *pro rata*. Thus, if ten actors perform before five hundred spectators one "day" of labor-time, each actor should be cred-ited with his day; total ten days; and each specta-tor charged with two-hundredths of a day, or two "strives" in average labor time currency.

14. That the share or proportion of a man's pro ducts or labor which is appropriated to reward help-ers, so far as that portion is not specially due to any other person, should be, if he is married, credited to his wife, and be subject to her free disposal. If their children help them, a dividend from the helper's fund credited to the father and mother should be set apart for the children.

15. That there should be levied on every amount credited to any and every person, a *pro rata* tax for

educational purposes; but the State should have no control of the tax, except to collect it; and when collected, to distribute it according to this rule: That parents might associate, select a teacher, determine what text-books should be used by him, and draw on the school fund in favor of the teacher for a *pro rata*, according to the number of children and actual labor-time consumed in teaching them; the State having no inspection of the school except to see that the amount of the draft is honest and correct.

My children: Beware of imitating the laws of Nodland which permit and secure titles acquired in perpetuity by prescription, accession, sale, exchange, hire, rent, treasuretrove, preoccupancy, capture, salvage, usury, etc. Beware, therefore, of allowing one or many from working for wages at a specific *per diem*, for a master or hirer who may insidiously undertake to bear the loss in order to appropriate to himself the gain that may result from any combination of *help*. Be vigilant in requiring that all help, all personal service, shall he recompensed by its proper share or proportion of the average labor-time value or price of the thing produced by the individual, the company or corporation helped or served. Have no masters and wagemen among you; but only associates or families. "Be not *you* called masters, for *one* only is your master, and all you are brethren." (Matt. x. 8.)

Never forget that no man can get rich by his isolated, his unaided labor. That exceptional riches is only acquired by one who sells natural values which belong to all, or by one who appropriates the difference gained by combined manual or instrumental labor which is done by many, and which should be divided among the co-operators. Remember that capital must, in each instance, be traced to its real producers, and that their proportionate share of it must be secured to them respectively.

To do this you must ever bear in mind the fact that there is in all things a natural or intrinsic value which

10

is God's share; but which the children of Cain, to avoid naming the true owner, designate by the phrase " value in *use*," and subordinate to their many-sided and aleatory "value in *exchange*."

We in the Eden of Labor have no title to things in themselves, but only to the labor-time we have respectively embodied in the things we respectively possess.

Hence we have—

1. Property containing only the individual labor-time of the possessor; *id est*, property which he has alone produced or which has been set apart for him or drawn by him as his portion of a common product, or which has been paid for by him from the dividend of *his own* labor-time. This he disposes of or consumes at will. It is ordinarily food, clothing, utensils; goods, chattels, or provisions which may be used or consumed by a *single* person.

2. Property produced by help, a *combined* effect of the division of labor, the specific outcome of a machine worked by more than one person, property produced by the joint or concerted labor of several or many, property bought by the labor-time money-notes contributed by several or many. Such as this is necessarily partnership property, and should be used, disposed of, and consumed as such, with due regard to proportion of labor-time contribution so long as it remains undivided.

3. Property owned by the State, or communities, or companies, but entrusted to individuals or corporations for some private or separated use or purpose. These are generally improvements of farms or factories, or machines, or ships, and so forth, advanced to new companies, or dwellings built by the State or community out of the common building fund. For these *no rent* is ever required, but only the repairs and restoration due by a "borrower for use;" that is to say, he must keep and restore the thing in good order, without tribute or increase, and without bearing the loss consequent on natural decay or excusable

accident, that is to say, he must restore only the portion of labor-time, value, or price he has EX-TRACTED *from the* THING by his use of it, but not what he has *produced* by that use.

Since price is measured or pay exacted especially and only for average labor-time, it follows that a private individual, or set, or company, or class of persons, cannot take or acquire, *apart from the rest*, of the community, the extra gain or abundance resulting from (1) labor saving machines, (2) the co-operation of particularized labor, (3) richness of soil, or (4) from excellence of quality. These, therefore, will inure to the benefit of the whole community—the work people in general. Hence it also follows that the greater the product, the more prolific lands, machines, and co-operations may happen to be, the greater the abundance produced by a given amount of labor, in any instance more than in another, the greater will be the dividend, not merely of the operatives of the extra prolific instance, but of all who labor. The sum total of these extra benefits it is our duty to divide *pro rata* to the labor-time of each member of the whole body of workers. It is God's portion, and should be distributed to all his children by an unselfish rule.

Thus you see, my dear children, we have sales and exchanges, barter, commerce, traffic, distribution, but make *no profits*.

We have dwellings, lands, machines, which we do not own, have not paid for, and which the isolated labor of the users could never pay for; but as the tenants or possessors thereof pay *no rent*.

We have money—our labor-time currency—which is advanced or loaned in case of need, or on occasion of a development of necessary or commodious production; but we cannot require the borrower to return increase. We permit *no usury*.

We have helpers, personal service and the like, but only as co-operators, members of families, brethren sharing the fruits of contributive labor-time ; but *no wagemen nor wages.*

Withal every one is rewarded for his labor according to the true ratio it bears to that of any and every other man.

My children : Maintain the practical rules and regulations by which these results are obtained, and you will thereby secure temporal abundance and enjoyment to all; but observe that this social order and happiness rests upon religious faith, and the consequent recognition of human brotherhood, and of the Divine title to all natural or inherent values.

CHAPTER VII.

NODLAND; ITS LANDLORDS AND TENANTS.

THE first dissension that ever arose between men probably had its origin in the first "division of labor." This first division was the parting of pastoral from agricultural labor. If labor is sundered into distinct avocations, discordant interests may be created, and then occasions of hostile collision will arise between them. The cattle of Abel, the shepherd, no doubt, despite every precaution, sometimes overran the fields of Cain, the husbandman. A deadly enmity arose in the heart of the latter; and this had culminated when the Searcher of Souls rejected Cain's sacrifice. Having slain his brother, Cain fled from the face of his father and nephews; but he repented of his sin; and hence was mercifully forgiven and protected. It would seem, also, that this divine protection, manifested by a mark or sign indelibly imprinted on his person, had a further significance. It was a figure of the future course of providence. The fulfilment of the divine decree that man should till the ground could not be waived. Man was not to be permitted to live by means of pasturage alone. Metaphorically, we may say that Cain's murder of Abel was Agriculture killing Pasturage and Herding. A similar doom has befallen pastoral labor in all ages and countries. Husbandry overcomes and destroys Pasturage whenever and wherever the latter attempts to stay in the neighborhood of cultivable lands. In every instance of contact, whatever momentary success Pasturage may achieve, Husbandry finally gains a definitive supremacy. The Husbandmen, with the divine protection, have always been able to possess the rich lands, and the Herdsmen have always been

10*

forced to confine themselves to stony hills, or to
perish entirely. Abraham emigrated to rocky parts
of Canaan. Jacob, persecuted by Esau and the
Canaanites of the valleys, was driven by them from
an arid place here, to a more arid place there.
Finally, reduced to starvation, he emigrated to
Egypt to seek bread and become the servant of an
agricultural people. After many struggles, pasturage has nearly disappeared in Europe. At this very
moment, the landed aristocracy of England and Ire-
land are threatened with evil for their obstinacy in
devoting large tracts of arable land to pasturage.
The raising of cattle on large and rich pastures in
America has been gradually forced to recede from
the East, and move to the plains of the Far West
and Texas. Even there it is not allowed to rest;
for, there also, the tillers of the soil (who were
obliged to fence in their fields against the roaming
cattle of their predecessors) now claim to be dispensed from making inclosures. They require that,
on the contrary, it shall be made the duty of the
cattle-raisers to have fences to keep their beasts from
roving, so that, as in all thickly cultivated countries,
a mere ditch or fringy hedge may be the only needed
boundary of an agricultural farm.

This account of the shepherds or herdsmen applies
to the huntsmen, with the difference, that the herdsmen were at one with the tillers in regarding the
huntsmen as common enemies. Hence we read of
Ismael, the *archer*, or huntsman (Gen. xxi. 10), that
his hand was against all men and all men's hands
were against him (Gen. xvi. 12).

It is remarkable that the herdsmen were not the
first weavers, though they were the producers of the
wool. Their nomadic life was not favorable to progress in the arts. Of the two classes the tillers were
the greatest inventors. The sons of the *husbandman*,
Cain, were famous for their ingenuity. The tillers
were permanently located, and therefore had every
inducement to improve their homes, and other fixed

capital — their implements and soil. They were stimulated by the greater yearly product of their labor, set to thinking by the greater complication of their pursuits, and on account of the numerous processes through which their products had to pass to be made fit for consumption. Wheat had to be ground, cotton spun and wove; the harvest when gathered must be stored and carefully preserved; they needed all the household instruments the herdsmen and huntsmen used, and must have many others which the nomads did not need; they required the same arms, if not for offence, at least for defence.

Living in close proximity to each other, the tillers enjoyed the great advantage of being ever able to unite for driving back a common enemy, and of building fortresses and other places of refuge and resistance. Hence, in their wars with the herdsmen, they were almost always victorious. A few great instances may be cited, in which the herdsmen were the conquerers; but in each case the sequel sustained the theory that agriculture is the providential destiny; for, the nomadic victors were soon compelled, by the force of circumstances, to cultivate the soil. The shepherd kings of Egypt found it necessary to make farmers of their common followers. The barbarian hordes, who subdued the Roman Empire, were soon, with the exception of their chiefs, obliged to throw aside the battle axe and mace for the plough.

Nor should we imagine that Cain, in the land of Nod, became a herdsman or huntsman. The history of his children shows that they must have been brought up to a very different kind of life. Certainly Cain was a fugitive and a wanderer, but this only in the sense that he fled from justice and wandered from the home of his father and brethren; for it is expressly stated that he *dwelt* in the distant land of Nod, a place of banishment, as its name implies; and that there "he built a city." The inference from all the facts is, that he founded a separate nation over which he ruled.

The laws Cain gave to his descendants and people were not inspired by the same sublime wisdom as those established by Adam for the Eden of Labor. Cain's laws, notwithstanding the deep remorse he felt for his fratricide, were tinged with the inequitable tendencies of his heart. He sanctioned the doctrine that all the land belonged originally and absolutely to the State; and that, therefore, the sovereign could give individuals a perpetual and transferable title, not only to improvements and actual uses, but to the natural thing itself. He allowed man to claim and hold, not as a mere *tenant* from God, but as ultimate owner. This, though Cain did not, perhaps, so intend it, was the origin of a wide spread perversion of the primary idea of economic justice; for this initial perversion led to others of the same kind, which, in the course of time, became the law of the whole earth; and transformed themselves into the iniquities and abuses that have been continued and maintained down to the present age.

Let us imagine the land of Nod as including the sources of the Indus, and of the confluents of that river; and as extending from thence to the shores of the Indian and Pacific Oceans. Probably Cain lived as long as Seth, and his family doubtless increased as fast, so that, before his death, it must have spread over nearly all this territory. As it put forth colonies, Cain allowed each of them to take possession of large tracts of country, and set bounderies to the portions they respectively desired to appropriate. To prevent disputes, he gave to the leader of each colony a patent, defining, as nearly as possible, the limits of the country it had appropriated; and this patent conveyed a perpetual title on the condition of the recognition of Cain's sovereignty, and of the payment to him of tribute, should he require it, to support his dignity, or to defray the expense of the public service.

For several generations this basis and form of title gave rise to no objection. On the contrary, it was

cheerfully accepted as natural and just. Was he not
the patriarch—their natural king? did not all men
by common consent bow to his authority? Besides,
was there not ground enough to supply the requirements of all, even to the extent of extravagant appropriation, and still to' leave what seemed an inexhaustible space for future population? None were
deprived, though the colonial chiefs, in a spirit of
cupidity and ambition, would always take land sufficient for a State. After several generations, there
still remained beautiful and fertile territories open
to emigration and settlement. Land commanded no
price; for every one could get from the State as
much as he wanted for nothing; and the title deed
given vested him, his heirs, or his or their assigns,
with absolute ownership *forever*.

Hence, by the decree of patriarchal power and
common consent, this system had been for centuries
the law of land-tenure before it gave occasion to any
serious inconvenience, or its fundamental violation
of God's title was even dreamed of. At last, however, the hardships it was bound to cause were felt,
though the primary wrong which had been perpe-
trated was not understood.

In the course of time population spread itself in
every accessible direction from the original centre.
This centre was thickly peopled; the territory immediately beyond it was less populous; the next still
less; and so the ratio of population to extent of
country went on diminishing; but, for hundreds of
miles, absolute title to the land had vested in somebody—the chief of a tribe or his grantees. To reach
the wild region beyond required months of irksome,
difficult, and expensive travel. Few had the strength,
courage, and means for this; yet to thousands emigration had become an imperious necessity. The
central area could not support the excessive number
of inhabitants that had grown up within it. They
must take refuge somewhere or die of starvation
among their brethren. Only one recourse was left.

It was for the poor to hire themselves to the owners
of lands in the less populous districts not too far
away; while those who had still a small amount of
dwindling capital could go a little further, and purchase a few acres from *preoccupants* who owned
much more than they could cultivate.

Thus the homogeneity of families was destroyed.
The members were separated; for, each had to seek
his fortune or bread wherever opportunity was presented, and they went in different directions to find a
home among strangers.

Every year this process repeated itself, until the
wave of surplus population came so near the unoccupied wilds that it could remove to them without too
much effort and outlay. But this, too, had its term.
Finally, the whole continent, to its verge, and even
the islands around it, teemed with human beings,
of whom millions were reduced to the *minimum* of
subsistence, to pauperism, and even to dire pestilence
and famine.

But I am too hasty. I must relate some of the
incidental circumstances of the career of the Nodlanders to this last condition.

The same process is being repeated just now, in
our own America.

The most fertile lands were, of course, the first
appropriated; but when these had all been taken up,
and the increase of population had created a greater
demand for cultivable soil, that of the second quality
was sought for, and bought or rented from the government or from private owners. Subsequently, and
for the same reason, land of the third quality was
required, and so on till every inch of ground, even
that which could yield merely the minimum of subsistence, had been taken up. As this process went
on, the market price of every grade of soil rose
higher and higher: so that, at the end, it was only
land of the lowest grades that could be had (as the
richest could once) for nothing, and this only on rare
occasions; for rich proprietors preferred to keep

their sterile acres vacant rather than be troubled by
poverty stricken neighbors, from whom they could
derive no rent or profit. Such lands yielded no surplus of crop with which to pay rent; but the others
did, and the owners failed not to exact it; and the
amount so exacted was always the whole product or
its value, except only so much as was necessary for
the bare subsistence of the laboring tenant.   Hence
the landlords took *all* the net or surplus product for
the use of their land.   It made little or no difference
how rich the land was; whether it yielded ten,
twenty, forty, eighty, or an hundred-fold, the share
left to the real producer, to him who had ploughed,
sown, and reaped, was never more than enough for
scanty—nay, miserable support.   The laborer could
not have and enjoy the fruit raised by his own hand.
It is easy to explain this.   On the one hand, there
lay the land wild, or at least idle; but it had a
human owner, who, though he could not cultivate it,
could (by virtue of a title primarily derived from
government) prevent all others from cultivating it.
His permission was necessary; and inexorably did
he exercise this dog-in-a-manger privilege till he had
stipulated the highest possible rent for waiving it
temporarily.   This rent he always found it easy to
obtain; for, on the other hand, there was always an
excess of poor husbandmen owning no land, each of
whom was anxious to get a lease even on the hardest
conditions, that they and their families might be
saved from exposure and starvation.   This unequal
competition with the engrossers of lands did not
come at once; but it was inevitable by the increase
of population.   In the beginning there was competition among the land-owners, and they left a large
part of the net crops to their tenants; but they raised
the rent with the demand till the rate reached the
maximum for the lessor, and the *minimum* from the
lessee.   Happy he who, in the mean time, had by
hook or crook secured the ownership of the soil he
was tilling with his own hand.   He at least enjoyed

comparative abundance during his lifetime. His children, however, hardly ever enjoyed this advantage; for if the farm was too small to be partitioned among them in kind, it was sold, to be divided in money. It was bought by those who had been accumulating capital from the surplus of crops they had obtained as rent of their lands. Thus the agricultural laborer was kept, without hope of redemption, at the lowest degree of poverty, while the capital of the landlord was continually accumulating. The product, and the capital of that moral entity called "the country," "the nation," was constantly increasing by millions and millions—*it*, the country, was therefore said to be prosperous and wealthy; but this had no real and tangible meaning except for the few who owned something—owned a share of this capitalized wealth. As to the real laborers, the national riches, no matter how hard or how skilfully they worked to produce it, did not exist. The fame of the country for its great riches seemed to the poor toiler to have been spread abroad to deride him. There was no difference to him whatever might be the enormous figure of this total abundance—no difference to him whether he tilled the ground as a tenant or as a wageman; the landlord always calculated rent or wages so as to take the entire net product.

This principle of rent (if such manner of rating can be called a principle) obtained also in cities and towns. As a town or city is enlarged by commerce and manufactures, its centre or grand artery is always determined by well-known circumstances. Population and business start from a centre, and spread from it, with reluctance, to less advantageous positions, and along the best roads leading to and from that centre, until the distance becomes inconveniently great. Then follows a lateral crowding of stores and dwellings. Finally, the urban area is densely occupied. This movement is closely followed—nay, anticipated in its course, by the prices of property and rates of rent, which advance in corresponding proportions. These expand, and bear relation in the same manner as do the prices and rents of rural property. They are influenced by the degrees of profitableness, by distance, and by other circumstances which determine the order of demand and occupancy. The indefeasible owners of lots and houses in cities observed the same rule for fixing the amount they thought it right to exact for rent or sale of their property that prevailed in the rural districts. They made the same and even greater profits. Such was the logical result of the character of their title, which, nevertheless, was always considered innocent and natural. None of them at the beginning, or afterwards, ever suspected its fundamental infirmity and wrong, and therefore acted as if it was perfectly valid and just before God. Hence, without reproach of conscience, they demanded and took the profit on labor it entitled them to have. Some became excessively rich. The least of them was also rich in comparison to the laborer who had no home of his own. It was with the landless workman our Lord Jesus Christ classes himself when he said, " The foxes have holes, and the birds of the air nests ; but the Son of man hath not where to lay his head." (Matt. viii. 20.)

Land speculation, its gains to its wily adepts, and its evil effects on labor, were consequences of this system. The speculators were of course persons who had accumulated capital from sales of original grants the State had made them, or from rents, or from some other lawful manner of appropriating all the share of God and the greatest share of labor in some natural thing or artificial product. These speculators studied the progress of population, and easily foresaw what would be the direction emigration would take, and what localities it would seek to occupy. Though this foresight was by no means singular or meritorious, the desire of deriving private gain from a movement of labor in which they did no share of work, was peculiar to themselves and their like. Over and over again, they seized these oppor-

11

tunities of enriching themselves at the cost of others, by employing their capital in purchasing lands, in those localities, either from government or from private owners who had preceded them, but were in want of money. Having thus forestalled or monopolized the soil, they pursued a Fabian policy towards the coming tide of population. At first they were liberal—their prices insignificant—they almost gave away a considerable number of farms to real settlers —to those who themselves would till the ground; but they (the speculators) reserved intermediate areas, and waited for the certain effects of the industry of the immigrants. The immigrants built houses, cleared tracts, planted fields, made roads to a market, established social security, and thus attracted less venturesome agriculturists and induced mechanics to settle among them. Then, for obvious reasons, alas! too familiar in practice, the privileged capitalist was able to sell or hire his land at an advance sometimes enormous. What did this unrighteous gain represent? It represented the labor of others—the effect of improvements made by a whole community —it represented a result that justly belonged wholly to that community or *pro rata* to its members, and in nowise to the idle and machiavelic land-speculator. He took, without doing a stroke of work, the reward due to the hardy pioneers who improved the wilderness and made it habitable. The same happened in urban situations. Labor came with her thousands of hands, turned villages into towns, towns into cities, cities into great emporiums; but the speculators, like birds of prey, hovered over all to snatch away, by artifice, and by virtue of a long sanctioned invasion of divine ownership, the benefits which labor alone is entitled to receive and enjoy.

I have supposed that in Nodland, Cain vested his sons with the first titles to definite districts of country —that this was the way in which the absolute ownership of land (as distinguished from actual laborious or usufructuary possession) originated. Some probably would prefer the theory of origin of title by pre-occupancy ; but that would make no difference in the consequences deduced. The nature of such a title implies real occupancy ; and it therefore cannot include what is not actually occupied, or last longer than the fact of occupancy. In other words, occupancy is occupancy, no more, no less ; but ownership is a great deal more, and even dispenses with real occupancy. Be this, however, as it may, certain it is that the pre-occupant, if we must so call him, invariably appropriated more land than he occupied, and claimed the uncultivated—the unoccupied excess by virtue of some mere pretence, or kept it for himself, against all comers, by force. He took, for a family, areas large enough for clans and tribes, and exacted a price for any vacant land others might need. If a stranger coming there to settle, was a chief having many servants and followers, he would occupy by force despite any pretext ; but if he was unable to avail himself of the right of might, he found himself under the necessity of purchasing and paying before he could have. Hence the same wrong is done by pre-occupants as by the State. Nevertheless I prefer the theory which traces the origin of fee-simple or absolute ownership to the State—a Patriarch, a Chief, a King, an Assembly ruling society and exercising sovereignty over a territory. In considering whether this theory be correct or not, we cannot regard the kind of title claimed by primitive herdsmen or hunters as proving anything ; for it was merely temporary and fixed no metes and bounds. The hunters and herdsmen were nomadic. None of them had a distinct possession. They had not even the intention of occupying any particular place permanently. We see this in the lives of Abraham, Isaac, and Jacob, who, though they expected a future generation of their race would own Canaan, had no notion that their transitory mode of occupying spaces of country gave them ownership as we understand it. What constitutes ownership is the setting apart, in perpetuity, a specific piece of land of defined limits, to an individual, his heirs and assigns. This takes place only among an agricultural people, organized under a government; and as far back as we have any record or tradition, the first titles were distributed and conceded by the State as primary owner and grantor.

Abimelech, king of Gerara, exercised this right of ownership (Gen. xx. 15) on occasion of the wrong done to Sara; and, on another occasion, though he was willing to give, he sold to Abraham, for seven ewe lambs, the spot where the latter himself had dug a well. The inference from the text (Gen. xxi. 30), is that a consideration given, and not a mere gift, conveyed a guaranteed title. Again, it was by means only of the payment of a price to the authorities of Heth, that Abraham obtained an individual title to the field and cave of Epron. (Gen. xxiii.)

It was a king of Mauritania, who sold the ground of Carthage to Dido; and ancient history contains a number of other instances of gifts, sales, and distributions of land made by the State, its kings and legislators, who, wherever the people were agricultural, appear to have been regarded as the original source of justice and land ownership.

Under the feudal system, the chief who had led the people to conquest, distributed lands among his followers, as prime owner of the conquered country; and they did him homage and service for their tenures.

When America was discovered, the European kings claimed ownership of the parts discovered by their subjects, and afterwards conceded whole territories to leaders of colonies, or tracts to individuals. Every private title to land, in America, is traceable up to the State.

Now, whence is the title of the State itself? Evidently it never acquired any; and could have none. Its only right would be in the assumption that it is the trustee of heaven, to award and regulate the use of the land for the common good. We have seen how it has fulfilled this obligation. It has, on the contrary, established a system of exclusive privilege in perpetuity—whereby titles pass to heirs and assigns forever independently of use or abuse, whereby the laborers and real producers are for all time condemned to pay extortionate tribute to fortunate, favored, and unproductive idlers.

11*

CHAPTER VIII.

MINES, MACHINES, WAGES, MONEY, AND FINANCE.

A STRIKING instance of the appropriation of God's share of natural things, for the exclusive benefit of exceptional individuals, is that of *mines.* We have seen how unqualified ownership of land is acquired and abused by the favorites of the State or the detainers of capital; and now I call attention to the fact, that sometimes these lands which have been thus unqualifiedly appropriated are found to contain mines. Hidden masses of coal, iron, copper, tin, lead, zinc, marble, sulphur, platina, silver, gold, etc., are here and there unexpectedly disclosed to the wondering and greedy eyes of the owner of a piece of ground. To whom does this newly discovered treasure belong? Still more than the cultivable soil it appertains to God's share. How should it be worked and its products disposed of? Clearly, for the common benefit of God's children.

But what did a Nodlander do when he discovered a mine on his estate? Only what the law of unqualified ownership authorized and sanctioned. He took possession of it as exclusive owner of the realty and its product. He hired hands to work it, paid them so much a day for extracting a quantity of metal worth many times more than the wages and other expenses. This was simply withholding and appropriating the largest part of the just earnings of labor. The idle non-producer took the lion's share of the capture—he took all the natural value, and the greatest part of the labor value. He counted his gains by millions; and invested them in acquiring title to other things and works producing similar income, on the same principle. The riches accumulated by the original appropriators of mines was enormous. Disposed to lead a life of amusement and luxury, and having superabundant means, they often determined to get rid of the care of watching their servants, and to avoid the trouble of taking possession of the values those servants laid at their feet. However, none of them ever thought of saying: "I have a million-fold more than my equitable share; I will extort no more from labor; I will let the laborers who have done this for me, extract the rest and share it among themselves according to their respective industry." No, they sought a new master to set him over the workman and continue the pressuration. For instance, they would sell a mine to a stock company for a very large sum. The stockholders or partners would commission an agent to conduct the work while they, though remaining idle, would draw dividends of profits derived from the labor of the toilers. According to the prevailing ideas of justice, these new owners expected to draw, from the working of the mine, not merely the ordinary interest of the money they had paid, but a large profit besides. Hence, the hardships of servitude were aggravated; for the mine had cost the original owner comparatively nothing, and he found it easy to pay liberal wages, but the new charges the new owners had to make on the labor product, in order to indemnify themselves and get gain besides, would expel all generosity from their hearts. Their first thought and first act after taking possession was to reduce the wages of their miners; and the poor fellows were compelled to work for the hopeless *minimum* necessary for bare subsistence. "We cannot afford to do better for you," was the peremptory and seemingly conclusive answer to all their remonstrances against such treatment.

Similar circumstances followed the introduction of machines.

The first machine ever invented (apart and beyond mere tools or implements) was what the political economists called the "Division of Labor," but which would be better named "The Association of particularized Labor;" for it is only when divided operations are associated and combined to accomplish a unit of product that the so-called "Division of Labor" is advantageous or even at all useful. For instance, the numerous hands, each having a particular operation to perform, in the manufacture of a newspaper, and who are each able to do the more work by having only that same operation to repeat, are not principally, but only incidentally divided. It is more proper to say they are associated. From the sheet-feeder or folder to the foreman, they compose a complicated *machine*, which multiplies production. By it ten men in *one* day are able to turn out many times more work than one man in twenty or even a hundred days, could turn out with the same appliances. Indeed, there are many works which could not be done at all without this combination of many in one. A single workman could not possibly build a house, or a ship, etc.; but when they combine in proper proportions of each art and section of art, the fabric is constructed in a few days. By this beautiful device or process, what would take years to do is accomplished in a few days. This effect is due to the artistic association; and therefore it follows that the workmen are entitled (if any one is) to whatever additional benefit or increase is procured by their combination. In Nodland, however, it was not so. If, for instance, a man who could not have built a house by himself in a hundred years, wanted one on his land, he would have it constructed by an "association of particularized labor." The work would be done in a few days and delivered. From that time the owner would enjoy the occupancy or the rent—suddenly receive a benefit which he could not have procured alone, and conferred only by the association. Nevertheless he would pay the workmen as if each had worked alone, as if there had been nothing accomplished by their working in unison, or by their co-adapting their skill and labor with artistic ingenuity and multiple efficiency. He would give each of them the minimum wages per day of an isolated laborer, and take the difference of time gained, the difference of revenue gained, all to himself; he who had done nothing but stand by and look down upon the wonderful power and effects of their co-operation.

It is almost a repetition to tell what happened from the introduction of mechanical contrivances that saved labor and multiplied its products. In the abstract, and regarding their intrinsic power of producing more with less labor, machines in themselves are good, are fruits of progress, pregnant with blessings to mankind : but when we observe how this potential beneficence is diverted, engrossed by individuals, and made an instrument for subjugating and oppressing those who work it, we are tempted to condemn the machines themselves instead of their appropriators.

There were patent laws in Nodland which conferred on inventors, for a term of years, the exclusive right to make, use, and vend the machines they contrived. Hence a valuable new improvement was like the discovery of a mine, only the inventor had merit which the discoverer had not. Nevertheless, as proprietors, they acted on the same principle. The inventive Nodlander, whenever his machine was found really advantageous (which by the by was hardly once in a thousand cases) would exact a "royalty" from labor for its use. Then he would sell his privilege at a great price to some capitalist or company of capitalists, greedy of gain, who would, to make that gain as large as possible, take advantage of competition to obtain workmen at the lowest possible wages; and avail themselves also of their monopoly to charge exorbitant profits on that labor to those who needed their machines. Before the expiration of their patents, they had time with these profits to establish large and very costly manufactories in which their machines could be made at so low a cost and in such quantities that they were able to defy competition. If an imprudent competitor did arise, they undersold him till they crushed him, and then put up their prices again.

As time went on the machines invented became (with a very few exceptions) more and more complex, in this particular that they were made to accomplish a greater number of the operations of a single art. It was as if an association of particularized labor were combined in the series of levers, wheels, cogs, screws, wedges, and belts; but the inventor or his assigns got a goodly share of the benefit, while combinations of brain and muscle producing like effects were allowed only the wages current, *per capita*, for disassociated service. Association of insensible matter was encouraged and rewarded, but that of human beings brought no reward to the associates; it was confiscated by their employers.

These great machines were so costly that it required a large capital to make and use them. This capital (from causes already stated and other causes to be pointed out anon) was in the hands of the original appropriators of natural value, or in the hands of their successors. Hence the original usurpation of natural values was perpetuated in a new form; or rather, the appropriators, by means of their capital, obtained control of the new kind of property evolved by inventiveness, by genius, and by the progress of science and art. They took the cream and the cheese, and left the whey to labor. The clear product, from which only the minimum wages of labor had been strained, was their portion.

Of course the *commerce* of Nodland was contaminated by the vices of the proprietary system of the country. It was carried on with an intense spirit of selfishness. The fact that the appropriators of natural things could lawfully demand prices for them in excess of the value of the labor put into them, induced the determination of those prices by the caprice of variable desire or fashion, by the ever changing relative proportions of demand and supply, by the irregularly alternate successes of competition and monopoly, by the fears and hopes of money lenders, and the abuse of credit. Certainty and stability, continuity and regularity in the course of commerce, or in the business of those engaged in it, were impossible. The possibility of acquiring exceptional fortunes, excited cupidity, venality, and deceitfulness. A wide range was given to the greed of gain; for unlimited profit in the exchange of every kind of merchandise or other property was possible to those who could foresee, or guess, or stumble upon the winning side of the fluctuations which were continually occurring. Thus commerce, instead of being what was intended when it began, the avocation of men, who, for a fair remuneration, served as intermediaries and carriers between producers and consumers, became a career of adventure. It was as if a country of shifting scenes and moving landmarks, but full of hidden treasures, had been opened to the knight errants of fortune, who went there each to enrich himself alone, and who strove there each by practising some deception, or by taking advantage of some mistake to compass the overthrow and ruin of the others. But these adventures could not be undertaken without capital. Hence, when one was eager to go upon a commercial venture, but had no capital, he sought to borrow it from those who had already succeeded in accumulating gains from the labor products of land, of mines, and of machines, or from commerce itself; but the capitalist would not lend either merchandise or money without interest and security; and thus commerce, also, like land, mines, and machinery, became the vassal of capital. The mass of those who really performed the labors and accomplished the purposes of commerce, were allowed to share no part of the profits gained according to the system; but were mere wagemen hired by the day, month, or year, and sometimes by the job or piece. Need I say they were paid the smallest wages their competition for employment compelled them to accept? The man whose very business is to extract

gain from the labor of other men, though sometimes
he is liberal, is rarely so. It is inconsistent for him
to be generous; and, even when kindest, always re-
serves the principal portion of the profit, really made
only by his wagemen, to himself alone.

Much of the preceding account presupposes the
use of *money;* and it is time to state my version of
the causes of its introduction. The appropriation of
mines, lands, and all products above minimum wages,
was of course followed by sumptuous and luxurious
living among those who had secured the benefits of
this selfish plan of distribution. The wagemen had
nothing to exchange for the common and lowest products they consumed but their labor; and at first
they received those products, food, clothing, shelter,
and fuel, in kind. They received no cash, and
therefore could not buy anything from traders and
strangers. As between the members of the appropriating class, the case was different. They severally
dealt in only a few kinds of products, and sometimes
only in one. Therefore, each of them primarily possessed a large surplus of his peculiar commodity;
therefore, also, they were in need of one another's
products; and therefore, further, they made exchanges.
The owners of mines had only metals to barter, but
they soon perceived that these were much coveted.
Silver and gold were much sought after by the rich
appropriators, to make ornaments and utensils; but
these metals were scarce; and since the selfish system of Nodland gave full effect to *desire* and competition in the determination of values, this scarcity
enabled gold and silver mine owners to demand, for
their metals, the products of many times more labor
than those metals embodied. All those who had
other surplus commodities to spare, were willing to
give disproportionate quantities of their goods for
gold or silver, in order to be able to gratify their
vanity, by displaying these shining tokens of opu-
lence, on their persons, in the shape of diadems,
earrings, beads, bracelets, breast-plates, belts, and

other trinkets; or, on their tables, in the form of goblets, plates, dishes, spoons, and other household articles. These metals were soon recognized as being the most readily accepted by the wealthy possessors of other merchandise, and as having therefore the most general purchasing power. For a long time they circulated as a medium of exchange among the appropriators only; but at last the miners found it more convenient to pay their laborers in doles of metal, instead of subsistence in kind. The pay in determinate quantums of a fixed and unfluctuating circulating medium afforded more opportunities of changing wages, for they would reduce them whenever subsistence was cheap, but refuse to resume the former rate when provisions rose again. Thus instead of having the trouble and duty of providing substantial support in kind, they threw the burden of all advances of the cost of living on their servants; and seized the occasion of any decrease of this cost as a pretext for diminishing the weight of their own obligations. Soon this mode of rewarding labor was, of course, adopted by all other employers. Silver and gold, first in the shape of ingots, then in stamped coin, became the universal medium of exchange and standard of estimate. Thus popularized and adapted to a new and extensive use, money acquired a greater relative value. It finally became the seal and sanction of the cupidity of its primary appropriators; also, the embodiment and symbol of every encroachment of avarice aided by force and fraud, upon the rights of God and man. How true the words of St. Paul, "The desire of money is the *root of all evils*, which some coveting have erred from the faith, and have entangled themselves in many sorrows." (1 Tim. vi. 10.) If I had space I would quote the whole chapter; but pray turn to it, and study its application to the matter in hand.

If any commodity must be adopted as a common measure of value, under a system permitting the exaction of price for natural values, it is manifest that

12

gold is the best that could have been selected.   Any other commodity would be liable to the same objections that gold is, besides many other inconveniences and occasions of loss to which gold is not liable; but I need not dwell on this, for the point is familiar to every reader of political economy.   What I wish to note is, that money, in every form of circulating medium except the abstract labor-time for labor-time note of the Reductionese, is a synthesis and generator of conflicts of men, corruptions of mind, perversion of truth, pride of gain, temptations to sin, devilish delusions, and iniquitous desires, drawing or driving men to destruction and perdition. (1 Tim. vi. 9.)   Money, from its beginning, has been and now is the symbol and agent of every encroachment on the title of the Divinity to natural values.   It is a vehicle licensed to carry only Justice, but in which every iniquity has found a place.   It is a hieroglyph in which the expression of a ransom for that which costs nothing is blended and confounded with that of a just recompense of labor.   It serves to count, and nevertheless conceal, the price exacted for that which God has gratuitously furnished, and which he has given in trust or tenancy to all of us, for the purpose of being gratuitously distributed, if not used or consumed by the preoccupant.   It is the seal and exponent of all the conversions of natural things into absolute and perpetual property.

"Remember, O Lord, what is come upon us; consider and behold our reproach; . . . we have drunk our water for money; we have bought our wood." (Lam. v. 1 and 4.)

Among the consequences of the invention and use of MONEY, and of the commercial manners and customs of the Nodlanders, were aleatory credit, usury, banking, the use of paper evidences of debt as a circulating medium, the establishment of stock companies for banking, for insurance, and other investments of capital.   We have already seen how the venturesome undertakers of commerce sought credit and submitted to usury, making it necessary that their gains on labor should be the larger and larger, to overlap the interest and capital they were obliged to refund. But besides speculation in merchandise, there were other operations of credit that reduced the reward of labor and increased the wealth of the few privileged appropriators of its fruits.

It was perceived that rich capitalists would be the safest trustees or depositaries of uninvested accumulations of money, while, on the other hand, those who had acquired this confidence saw that they could turn it to their profit. They did this by accepting deposits restitutable on demand, but relying on the probability of there being constantly a proportion of the deposits remaining uncalled for, they did not hesitate to lend this proportion for usury. Thereby they made great gain from the use of funds belonging to others, and to the fruits of which they had no equitable right. It was not merely a reasonable charge for the trouble and service of *keeping* the money they made, but it was a violation of the nature of their contract they committed; and this even when they exacted pay for the *keeping*.

These depositaries were called bankers, and established correspondences in different cities, for the purpose of acting as intermediaries between debtors and creditors who might want to send and receive money balances to and fro. They invented the bill of exchange, for which (that is to say, the mere trouble of writing them, after receiving the cash for them), they took considerable premiums. Here, then, was another current running into the grand reservoir of the appropriators.

Eagerly searching for every means of unproductive profit, they studied with keen minuteness all the operations and investments of capital, and thus were able to ascertain that losses by fire, storm, and other accidents conformed to certain laws, and happened in certain proportions. On this knowledge they based the invention of insurance. They applied it even to

the chances of the loss of life Their reputed or real
ability to fulfil any promise for the payment of money
was of itself sufficient to induce others to pay them
premiums for their warranties against loss. Every
merchant and proprietor availed himself of their
policies. They professed to take risks, but their cal-
culations were made to secure to their customers the
payment of their losses, not out of the capital originally deposited for that purpose, but out of the very
premiums themselves. Hence while the customers
were really mutual insurers, the nominal guarantors,
or issuers of policies, realized enormous profits from
their paper contrivance, and thus another tributary
brought more drain from labor into the usurious gulf.
With a nominal capital of a million, they would insure five hundred millions of property. Judge what
an enormous aggregate of profit this must have
yielded. But not content with this, they calculated
they would have always a residuum of premiums not
needed to pay losses, and these of course they invested in loans, pledges, and stocks, thus increasing
their dividends of gain from the money of others.

By and by the large capitalists recognized the fact
that their notes were taken as readily as money. The
only obstacle to their general circulation was their
large and inconvenient amounts. Here they scented
a new and rich game. They invented the bank note
payable on demand, but which they cunningly foresaw
would remain outstanding and circulating a long time
before its redemption in coin would be asked. Hence
they could lend these notes as if they were real money,
and make their capital bring them returns as if it
were double or triple its real amount.

The play of this system enabled them to lend millions on millions to governments for war and public
works, and to corporations for railroads and other
industrial enterprises, though really paying out
hardly a tithe. They would make these enormous
loans in instalments, well knowing that the government or corporation would disburse the instalment

immediately, and that the creditors and others who
received the disbursements would bring them at once
back to the bank as a deposit, or for the purpose of
purchasing the very bonds the government or company had issued seemingly to procure funds to pay
them. They could act on this just as if they had not
paid the government a dollar. Often the bankers
and their constituents were themselves, in fact, the
present or anticipated creditors, who thus took bonds
at a heavy discount, which, however, they knew they
could make available at will for as much cash as
they had use for. They had reason to be confident
of being able to retail their bonds to small takers at
at advance before funds were required for a second
instalment of the loan. Besides, often a borrowing
government would, on the deposit of bonds on which
it was itself paying interest, enforce and guarantee
the circulation of the bank notes, and thus help to
increase the lending and operative power of their
usurious creditors.

Naturally small capitalists would try to imitate
this financial machinery; but to do so they were
obliged to club together and create stock companies,
which often enjoyed the same great credit as the
banks of the larger capitalists. Hence they too received deposits, dealt in exchange and bonds, dis-
counted notes, took pledges, issued paper money, and
underwrote policies, as if each company were a single
person; and they made similar profits. The main
point with them was to induce *real* depositors to trust
them with the keeping of capital which would not be
called for immediately. When they inspired sufficient confidence to bring this about, their success was
sometimes remarkable; but there was a drawback.
Their officers and members were often tempted to
enlarge their individual business and speculations,
and themselves became borrowers. The facility
their own bank afforded them, made them frequently
imprudent, so that they failed in business; and, when

12*

this happened, it would bring ruin to the bank as well as to themselves.

They used their depositors' money to enlarge the credit of the corporation. They loaned not only their depositors' money, but also the enlarged credit, derived from that money, to the depositors' rivals and competitors. An intoxicating and inflating stimulant was thus given to mere speculation. All normal business transactions were interfered with and entangled; and the regular current of trade was broken up into eddies, whirlpools, and overflows. Reckless of the external effects of their operations, they strained continually to multiply them, so long as their speculative borrowers did not fail and thereby make it necessary for them to contract. They rejoiced every time that, with apparent security, they could lend one of their notes, and every time the holder of a check drawn against them would, instead of demanding payment, leave it on deposit. Every such transaction added to their usurious profit.

One of the ways these borrowing bankers contrived, for searching out and getting hold of all the idle money in the country, was the pretext of savings banks. They would tempt the poor, by promises of interest and of safe investments, to bring the small residuum which, by dint of self-privation, was left of their wages. This they generally loaned to themselves, and thus obtained additional capital for speculation. If they prospered and enriched themselves, the poor got their money back with interest, but if their rivals outdid them, those rivals got all the poor man's savings, and he was reduced to greater hardships than ever.

As to canal companies and all other industrial corporations, they were, most times, a prey to the managing agents or undertakers of works or mortgagees. These were generally the founders of the companies, which they succeeded in establishing, by persuading the government to subscribe bonds, and hopeful persons to take stock. Then they would take the management of the enterprise; and thereby be able to involve it by onerous contracts with their confederates. It would of course declare no dividends, the stock would fall to almost nothing, and they could gradually buy it all up. They would thus make large profits on their private contracts, and use these same profits to become, for a comparative trifle, sole owners of all the shares of stock, and therefore of the franchise and its property.

CHAPTER IX.

Reign of Enos.

ABOUT the year of the world 937, and after the death of Cain, Enos, his son, the corrupt of soul and body, reigned over Nodland. In the Eden of Labor Enoch, the trained son of God, ruled as Supreme Patriarch; for both Adam and Seth were dead. The reign of the worthy successor of Cain lasted for more than a century; and during his time the consequences of the social policy of the prototype of fratricides was fully developed.

The reader has, perhaps, already inferred that the effect of the property laws of Nodland was to divide its people into classes or castes. Such, indeed, was the necessary effect, practically, if not ostensibly.

Shortly after ascending the throne, Enos conceived the design of creating a nobility, a privileged class, chosen from the natural defenders of the state craft of his father, whom he exceedingly admired. To form a clear idea of how this might best be done, and whom to choose for the rank and dignities he intended to confer, he caused an elaborate census of the population and resources of the country, occupations and fortunes of the people to be made.

When the commissioners of this census had tabulated their researches, the logical effects of the selfish system I have described were exhibited. The population had necessarily and tacitly resolved itself into several divisions, plainly discernible by many signs. The voluminous report of the commissioners proved the fact to be inherent to the constitution of the state. They made it evident by means of the minutest details, and well-grounded generalizations.

A schedule of these ascertained castes which I have extracted from their report, will, no doubt, be useful and interesting. I therefore make a copy of it for the benefit of my readers.

SCHEDULE OF CASTES.

FIRST GENERAL DIVISION: LORDS AND GENTRY.

1. MONEY LORDS. This class comprised those who had a large amount of capital, and were entirely free from debt—had no business establishment and no occupation but recreation, and had invested their capital in affairs managed by others, viz., the holders of millions worth of stock in canal, banking, and other companies; also "commendam" shares in commercial and industrial partnerships, investments in state loans, etc.

2. MONEYED GENTRY: those who had considerable, or even very large, funded capital of their own, but who *attended personally* to its administration and investment in bonds, stocks, mortgages, pledges, bills of exchange, loans to governments, and other securities. They also took charge of and managed the investments of the money lords. They were commonly called bankers.

3. LANDED GENTRY: those whose capital consisted principally of mines, farms, and houses, which they personally attended to, either by working the mines or farms on their own account on a large scale, employing laborers, etc., for that purpose; or by renting out their mines, farms, and houses, and collecting the rents directly from their tenants, in products or money.

4. MANUFACTURING GENTRY: those who were sole or principal owners of factories, founderies, mills, printing and publishing offices, brick-

yards, tanneries, distilleries, breweries, etc., which they personally superintended, and in which they employed many clerks, writers, reporters, pressmen, machinists, and other workmen, servants, or wagemen. The money lords often took shares or invested as silent partners in these establishments when they were carried on by stock companies.

5. MERCANTILE GENTRY: those who invested their own unborrowed capital in commercial adventures, were owners of stores, hotels, and inns, warehouses, lumber yards, and other merchandise; ships and vessels for transportation or fisheries, roads, canals, and other vehicles of common carriage, etc. etc., which they personally superintended, used, or disposed of in the course of trade, and in which they employed many clerks, workmen, and other wagemen.

6. SMALL CAPITALISTS: those who, while they belonged essentially to one or several of the above mentioned classes, operated with their own unborrowed, but inconsiderable capital. They were well-to-do planters, gardeners, distillers, brewers, builders, and contractors, livery-stable keepers, liquor dealers, eating-house keepers, slaughter-house keepers, machinists, smiths, printers and publishers, shipwrights, sugar refiners, founders, traders, and dealers in all kinds of merchandise, who carried on *a business of inferior size*, and who employed clerks, workmen, and other wagemen.

[*The essential characteristics of these six classes were* —1st, *they invested their own unborrowed capital;* 2d, *employed servitors for wages;* 3d, *exacted a price for natural values; and,* 4th, *extracted usury, rent, or profit from the labor of others.*]

SECOND GENERAL DIVISION: INDEPENDENTS.

7. INDEPENDENT PROFESSORS of science, art, and fine-art: those gifted with peculiar skill, talent, genius or inventiveness, and who required distinct and specific pay or fees for each special service they rendered. These were lawyers, doctors, authors, inventors, painters, musicians, sculptors, architects, experts, designers, star-actors, star-dancers, dentists, lecturers, engineers, short-hand writers, and all other professors and artists who did not serve others on time, or were not under obedience to masters and employers.

8. INDEPENDENT HUSBANDMEN: those who cultivated their own land *alone* or in partnership, and sold such products thereof as they did not themselves consume, and who did not hire wagemen to assist them. Home fishermen and huntsmen should be added here.

9. INDEPENDENT ARTISANS: those who carried on a manufacturing business, alone or in partnership, doing piece-work on their own account, for their own customers, or selling articles of their own make directly to the consumers, and who did this without the assistance of hired workmen of their own trade, or of other wagemen. In this class there were single-handed operatives of many kinds; bakers, barbers, and hair dressers, blacksmiths, book-binders, boot and shoemakers, butchers, cabinet-makers, carpenters and joiners, confectioners and pastrymen, engravers, gilders, dress-makers, milliners, gunsmiths, locksmiths, painters, paper-hangers, plasterers, printers, plumbers, rag-pickers, roofers and slaters, tailors, tinners, upholsterers, wheelwrights, and generally all kinds of petty jobbers who worked single handed.

10. INDEPENDENT HUCKSTERS: those who carried on a small *commercial* business, alone or in partnership, without the assistance of clerks or other wagemen. In this class there were tradesmen and operatives of many kinds; auctioneers, brokers, draymen, hackmen, packers, pawn-brokers, peddlers, weighers, gaugers, measurers, wagoners, retailers of every kind of goods, wares, and commodities, etc. etc.

[This general division had all the characteristics of that of the lords and gentry, except one; they did not hire others to work for them.]

THIRD GENERAL DIVISION: VASSALS.

11. TRIBUTARY HUSBANDMEN: all those agriculturists who might be classed in the first or second division, were it not for the fact that they had borrowed a part of their capital by mortgaging their land or had otherwise obtained credit, and were *paying usury* to their more thrifty or lucky compeers, or to the money lords and gentry.

12. TRIBUTARY FARMERS: laboring agriculturists who were cultivating lands which belonged to others, as lessees or tenants of the owners, and *paid rent* in money or in kind.

13. TRIBUTARY MANUFACTURERS: those who could be classed under one of the heads of the preceding divisions were it not for the fact that they had borrowed a part of their invested capital, and were *paying usury* to their more thrifty or lucky compeers, or to the money lords and gentry.

14. TRIBUTARY FACTORY-FARMERS: those who did not own, but *paid rent* for the whole or part of the factories they carried on, or for the machines they used.

15. TRIBUTARY TRADESMEN: those engaged in commerce and who would belong to the first or

second division, were it not for the fact that they had borrowed a part of their invested capital, and were *paying usury* to their more thrifty or lucky compeers, or to the money lords and gentry.

16. TRIBUTARY STORE KEEPERS AND CARRIERS: those who did not own, but *paid rent* for the whole or part of the store houses, warehouses, vessels, or vehicles, they used in carrying on their business.

17. TRIBUTARY HOUSEHOLDERS: those who, though free in other respects, *paid rent* for the private dwellings they occupied.

18. FICTITIOUS CAPITALISTS: those of this general division who carried on business with *no* capital but that which they borrowed, and for which they *paid usury.*

FOURTH GENERAL DIVISION: WAGEMEN OR SERFS.

19. SUPERIOR OFFICIALS: salaried executive, judicial and other civil magistrates, governors, judges, clerks of court, sheriffs, coroners, State counsellors, and public prosecutors, mayors, notaries, recorders, justices of the peace, etc.; also, officers of the army and navy. I include only those who had not the fortune required to belong to the *first* general division. There were many who had this. The heirs and relatives of the lords and gentry, generally held the higher and best paid offices.

20. ARTISTIC AND SCIENTIFIC WAGEMEN: professors, school-masters and other teachers, actors, musicians, acrobats, equestrians, dancers, and the like, who hire themselves by the day, week, month, or season, and are under obedience to their employers.

21. AGRICULTURAL WAGEMEN: ploughmen, reapers, dairymen and women, gardeners, nurserymen,
13

drovers, herders, apiarists, and others serving master agriculturists for wages.

22. MANUFACTURING WAGEMEN: machanics, millers, editors, and generally those enumerated in the *ninth* class, but who serve master employers for wages, whether on time or by the piece.

23. COMMERCIAL WAGEMEN: clerks, salesmen, messengers, porters, carmen, brakesmen, watchmen, bookkeepers, tellers, sailors, boatmen, lightermen, canalmen, packers, stablemen, captains, supercargoes, pilots, steamboat-men, stewards, toll-gatherers, collectors, conductors, weighers, gaugers, measurers, samplers, and other employés serving in the business of masters engaged in commerce, and who are paid wages on time or task for their services.

24. DOMESTIC SERVANTS: cooks, waiters, hostlers, coachmen, footmen, chambermaids, washers and ironers, butlers, seamstresses, and the like, who were not members of the family, but served for wages.

25. INFERIOR CIVIL OFFICIALS: deputy-sheriffs, constables, policemen, detectives, watchmen, inspectors, deputy clerks of courts, city firemen, and the like, whose services were paid by fees, or time wages, fixed by law.

26. INFERIOR MILITARY OFFICIALS: common soldiers, seamen, and marines, enlisted for a term, subject to obey orders implicitly, and supported on fixed rations and pay.

FIFTH GENERAL DIVISION: OUTCASTS.

27. PAUPERS: such as beggars, the destitute consigned to poor houses, or admitted permanently to asylums and houses of refuge, where they are provided with subsistence.

28. CRIMINALS: such as thieves, forgers, vagrants, swindlers, prostitutes, gamblers, and the like; also, generally all persons convicted and undergoing imprisonment for felony.

The number of people belonging to each division and class was shown by this census. For instance, the census of the oldest Province of Nodland, which had a population of forty million, showed, on careful analysis, the number of souls under each division to be as follows :—

FIRST DIVISION :
     1st Class : *Money Lords,* their wives and children   100,000
     2d to 6th Classes : *Gentry,*   "   "   "   900,000
SECOND DIVISION :
     The four classes of *Independents,*   "   "   3,000,000
THIRD DIVISION :
     The eight classes of *Vassals,*   "   "   5,000,000
FOURTH DIVISION :
     The eight classes of *Wagemen,*   "   "   30,000,000
FIFTH DIVISION :
     The two classes of *Outcasts* of both sexes and all
        ages   1,000,000

                                                     40,000,000

Approximately, this was the case in every one of the Provinces of Nodland. It thus appeared that the proportion of Money Lords was one in four hundred; that of the Gentry, nine in four hundred; that of the Independents, thirty in four hundred; that of the Vassals, fifty in four hundred; that of the Outcasts, ten in four hundred; and that of the Wagemen, three hundred in four hundred, or three-fourths of the whole population.

The Enosian census, compared with previous data, showed an increase of wagemen, paupers, and criminals, and a corresponding decrease of the other classes   It was not that none of the wagemen ever rose to the better-portioned rank of vassals, or even as high as that of money lords; or that none of the money lords, gentry, independents, or vassals ever descended to the grade of wagemen, or even of paupers; but, for many manifest causes, those who fell from affluence into bankruptcy and poverty were more numerous than those who ascended from serfdom to the domination of wealth. While *a few* wagemen, taking advantage of some exceptional skill

or talent they had acquired, or genius God had
blessed them with, would be able to obtain a large
remuneration from the rich, who, for the sake of
pleasure or profit, would avail themselves of that
skill, talent, or genius, at the same time *many* of the
money lords and gentry would squander all they
possessed in extravagant display or ruinous investments—speculations in stock, and so on. While
some of the vassals, taking advantage of opportunities—such as a new outlet of trade, the introduction
of a new fashion or invention, the development of a
new source of production, or the means of supplying
a demand of any kind at less cost—would thereby
realize large gains, free themselves from debt, and
become clear capitalists, *many more* would commit
mistakes in the choice of their adventures, make
false estimates, and act on delusive anticipations,
and hence would be disappointed, make losses instead
of profits, and sink into penury. While some independents, seizing the occasion of a run of custom,
would hire wagemen to help them, and succeed in
turning their little shops or stalls into factories and
stores representing considerable net gains, *a larger
number* would miscalculate the proportion of outlay
and income, or the duration of the profitable custom,
and hence would, at last, become hopelessly insolvent.
In every rash undertaking the covetous aspirant
would strain his credit, borrow money, give pledges,
mortgages and security to the lenders, pay away his
profits in usury, till he could pay no more; and
then see the usurers take away the property itself on
which they had made the loans. Thus, though the
number of the rich was constantly diminished, the
amount of the capital they absorbed and accumulated
constantly augmented; *the sum total of wealth was constantly becoming greater, while the participants were
constantly becoming less numerous.*

In such a society I hardly need to say wealthy persons were in high esteem; and the respect with which
one was treated, the influence and power he exercised,

was in proportion to his fortune. This discrimination was so marked that, though there was no legal distinction of castes, it really existed; and by common consent practically prevailed. Indeed, one might always know to what caste a man belonged by his personal appearance; his dress, his manners, his degree of cleanliness, and other *indicia*. The moneyed, landed, manufacturing, and commercial aristocracy were distinguishable by their luxurious style of living, their equipages, their supercilious deportment, and other modes of displaying their riches. As the scale of fortunes descended, it was generally easy to detect a graded diminution of sumptuousness and arrogance, or reserve, till, at last, with the wagemen all appearance of superiority vanished, to give place to humility, sordid apparel, coarse manners, and rough skins.

There was a clear demarcation between the wagemen and the other classes, not only in external appearance, but in the more serious matter of social antagonism. With the exception of the superior officials, who were generally parasites of the appropriators, there was an insuperable social barrier between the classes of wagemen and wage-payers; a continual antagonism between them, carried on most always silently, but tacitly understood, on both sides, to be irrevocable. The capitalists would, it is true, compete with each other in trade, speculation, and adventure, but they acted in unison on one point: *keeping down the wages of labor.* They were unanimous and firm in repressing any demand of the wagemen for any remuneration above the minimum of subsistence. On the other hand, it was the general desire, if not the active undertaking of the wagemen, to obtain more just and sufficient compensation; but circumstances and pusillanimity prevented a determined and united enforcement of their wish. They were distracted by dissentions and treason. A great number, actuated by the fear of hunger and an exclusive care for self, were continually betraying their

brethren, and underbidding the current rate of wages
to obtain employment. It often happened to them
that to fail in getting work and wages was to fail in
getting bread the next day for themselves and families. The appropriators had stores of provisions and
money—had no such fear of famine; and thus enjoyed an advantage which, even when the wagemen
were united, generally overcame their utmost perseverance. There was *no work or wages to be had, except such as the appropriators were able and willing to
give*, and of this there was hardly ever enough for
all the wagemen, so that the latter, in their struggles
to obtain it, were like shipwrecked persons in the
deep, clinging to an over crowded raft, or fighting
each other for a foothold upon it. Happy the laborer
when labor was in demand, laborers few, and employers competing for their service; but, alas! this
scarcely ever took place.

The partition, or distribution and consumption, of
the net products of industry, was entirely under the
control of the appropriators; and they divided it
among themselves, leaving only the crumbs for the
wagemen, who were doomed to take this or nothing.

This brings me to a set of facts which should be
carefully noted in every mind. I call particular
attention to them; for, without understanding them,
the reader will not understand the political economy
of Nodland, nor the events of its history that depended upon that political economy.

(1) Capital, in Nodland, was correctly distinguished
as being of two kinds, (1) productive, and (2) unproductive; and these again were either fixed capital,
which consisted of lands, buildings, machines, and
other long lasting property; or "circulating" capital, which consisted of the movable and, to a great
extent, rapidly perishable products of the last and
few preceding years (such as provisions, materials,
clothing, and other commodities and merchandise;
also interest of money, rents, and profits) remaining
unconsumed by incorporation in permanent property

or waiting to be consumed, unproductively or reproductively. The value and quantity of each of these
species of capital, however great, was *definite;* that
is to say, did not exceed some positive amount whether
known or unknown. All of it, even the permanent
kind (except the land, and even that to a great extent),
was: Firstly, consumable and destructible; and secondly,
from the total value and quantity of production being
limited *the increase of one kind necessarily implied the
decrease af another in any given state of labor power.*

(2) All capital or all labor was not essentially of
one or the other of these kinds. Some of it was
essentially of one or the other species, as food, which
is by its nature productive ; or as tobacco, which is
intrinsically unproductive; or as gardening, which in
itself is productive; or play-acting, which is inherently
unproductive. But, to a great extent, capital and
labor may be productive or unproductive *according
to the manner* it is used, or the *purpose* for which it is
consumed; as money, which may be used to buy
bread or a trinket; or as plowing, which may serve
for preparing a field for grain, or for levelling a lawn
to beautify the foreground of a mansion.

(3) The appropriators were the owners and masters of all the fixed and nearly all the circulating
capital, owners of the land, machines and bread; and
therefore dictators of labor. Labor had no capital,
had only brains and muscle, which lay powerless till
employed and salaried or patronized by Capital.
Hence, it was the appropriators who decided what *proportion* of capital should be reproductively invested,
what proportion unproductively consumed, what portion should remain circulating, and what should become " fixed." They could direct labor to either or
any of these ends: starve it or feed it as they deemed
expedient or agreeable to themselves.

(4) Every appropriator determined, for himself,
in which of these catagories—fixed, circulating, productive, or unproductive consumption—he would put
whatsoever belonged to him. One adopted the policy

of reproductive investment, and was enriched. Another yielded wholly to the allurements of unproductive consumption, and was impoverished. The avaricious deprived themselves, and sought only gain. The prodigals indulged themselves, and devoured or wasted all their substance. Few, however, pursued either policy absolutely. Generally they would each consume his income both productively and unproductively, and in various proportions, one differing from the other; but the inclination of the great majority of the appropriators was to enjoy themselves —display sumptuousness, revel in luxuries, seek pleasures — and thus consume unproductively the *greatest part* of their income, the largest portion of the net product of the labor of the wagemen.

(5) The appropriators generally expended most of the increase, and sometimes much of the principal, of their fortunes in such a manner that the cost of what they consumed excessively outweighed what would have been the cost of commodities equally comfortable and useful had they chosen and encouraged these. They preferred finery, ornaments, toys, equipages, palaces, balls, feasts, idle travel, and the thousand other ways of spending capital or net products destructively. The effect, of course, was to give a great impetus to the *production of unreproduc tive things*—of things which did not serve to give or renew strength, health, comfort, or intellect; and which furnished no power to supply or restore their like through consumption, but which in each instance were consumed once and irredeemably.

(6) True, a part of the price or cost of these things —the part paid to the wagemen who made them— served to sustain life and renew strength; and so far, but so far only, the appropriators furnished out of their resources reproductive commodities to the wagemen; but this was only to enable the wagemen *to replace the same vain and unfruitful things* which had been unproductively consumed. Hence the condition of the wagemen remained the same.

They could not purchase the fruits of their own labor with the wages of that labor. They maintained, or, if you will, even increased the wealth of the world, but not for themselves; not so that enough could be made for them to participate therein, except to a disproportionately small extent. They were as in a tread-mill, grinding out abundance of the costliest kind for the appropriators, but only a dole of miserable subsistence for themselves. They were prevented from producing an abundance of things "good for the poor," and affording them an enjoyable life.

(7) Thus, since capital and income were not unlimited, but, on the contrary, of a positive amount, and the tendency was towards the production of a maximum of unreproductive capital and a minimum of reproductive capital, the more the appropriators gathered or cut out of the labor of the wagemen, the less, in proportion, remained for productive re-investment. *There was a continual diminution of the proportion devoted to the production of necessary and commodious things;* and a progressive diverting of capital used to supply the wants of the wagemen, in order to invest it to gratify the desires of the sumptuous and vicious.

(8) Labor-saving machinery, discoveries of science, devices of inventive art, were preferably applied to increase the kind of production which the appropriators exclusively consumed. Their power of consumption of these things was limited only by the extent of their capital and revenues; but these were great, and they could make purchases and exchanges in a liberal manner with each other. On the other hand, the wagemen were limited to their wages, and these were so mean that they could only purchase necessary things at prices that yielded small profit. No wonder, then, that *the manufacture of unreproductive luxuries was stimulated.* Thus, while science and art were continually discovering and inventing ways of dispensing with human labor, they directed the

main current of the enormous *remainder* towards the production of luxuries. Hence, the number of persons needed for the new and luxurious manufactures were integrally more numerous, while the sum total, demanded for all work, was proportionally and progressively falling off. The capital and labor invested in the production of food, clothing, and shelter for the poor were reduced. The appropriators would invest in production of this kind only so far as it was necessary to supply the workmen they employed. Hence, the reduction was of the number of wagemen that produced commodities of the necessary kind. Thousands were thrown out of employ, and the consequent competition brought on reductions of wages. Pauperism and misery spread among the masses; and induced many diseases, epidemics, and excessive mortality, as if to restore the equilibrium between population and subsistence.

(9) But the real nature of the disturbance of equilibrium was between the reduced demand of the appropriators for reproductive labor on the one hand, and the increase of the excluded number of those offering to do that kind of labor on the other. If the appropriators had been willing, or their system of political economy had permitted, there would have been abundance of subsistence raised and made for a much larger population. Hence to a great extent, under their policy and caprice, the insufficiency of work, wages, and subsistence was independent of population. *Even in a sparse population*, the rich can, *without employing* ALL *those who are destitute of capital*, determine the application of land, machines, and money mainly to supplying more and more luxuries inaccessible to the poor. In such a case, alas! too frequent, it is clear that those whose services they determined to dispense with were doomed to compulsory idleness, misery, disease, and death. Judge what the effect must have been in a thickly populated country such as Nodland was.

(10) What the appropriators wanted was abundance

of all kinds of sumptuous articles and luxurious commodities, cheap enough for themselves even though
too costly for the wagemen. The appropriators had
power to direct their capital to this result, and did
so. Capital pleased itself first, and Labor, under
penalty of exclusion from the table of life, found
itself under the necessity of obsequiously seeking to
please Capital. The appropriators would not part
with enough wage money or necessary commodities
to support the numbers of the poor except on the
tacit condition that the majority of the poor must
devote their labor to the sumptuous and pleasurable
things or services in which they, the appropriators,
delighted. To enjoy these excellent things was the
motive of their extortion; the only motive of their
accumulation of capital, their only motive for furnishing work and wages to the poor. Hence the
poor were forced to produce luxuries, vanities, fashions, finery, amusements, shows, and even pander to
vice in order to live. These were almost exclusively
consumed by the rich. Nearly all that could be
saved or reserved out of labor in excess of absolutely
necessary subsistence, was invested in this way. Out
of the residue left to them the wagemen were hardly
ever able to make any savings. When they did make
any saving, the amount was pitiful, and they were
able to set it apart only by rigorously depriving
themselves of every comfort. Few had sufficient
courage and patience to do this. *They were tempted
to imitate, in a miserable way, the example of the wealthy;*
and would spend all they could possibly spare, in
buying cheap and detestably inferior qualities of *pernicious* things, such as strong and impure wines, or in
gratifying a taste for low and demoralizing amusements, such as indecent buffooneries and balls, or
even games of chance.

These facts were scrupulously noted and tabulated
by the commissioners of the census. When they were
laid before king Enos, he at once prudently ordered
that they be withheld from the public, lest they might

furnish a clue to the causes of the poverty of the masses, and give rise to agitation for radical reform, or may be to revolution.

Among the tables thus withheld was a curious one which made a division of the eight classes of wage-men into four *transverse* categories which were denoted by distinctive titles, as follows: (1) refiners, (2) parasites, (3) fructifiers, and (4) creepers. They also stated the number of wagemen, women and children, belonging to each of these cross categories.

(1) The "*Refiners*" were those among the wage people of every trade or occupation who worked in producing such necessary and commodious articles as were usually consumed by the wealthy, also the makers of things and doers of service exclusively sumptuous.

(2) The "*Parasites*" were those who, among any class of wage people, were employed to subserve the intemperance, lust, vain display, and other vicious pleasures and wastefulness of the wealthy.

(3) The "*Fructifyers*" were those who, among any class of wage people, devoted their labor-time to making products and rendering services "good for the poor," and at prices cheap enough to be paid for out of their wages.

(4) The "*Creepers*" were those who, among any class of wage people, earned their subsistence by ministering, in any way, to the intemperance and other immoral habits of the poor.

The remarkable facts disclosed by this tabulation, and by the investigations required to fill it up, were these :—

That the wealthy would accept, for their own consumption, only articles or commodities, work or service of excellent quality; and which, therefore, involved an extra proportion of labor and skill; and, therefore, also required the best workmen and finest materials and products for their manufacture, so that *even* the necessary and commodious things they consumed—their food, clothing, houses, furniture, and fuel—were really sumptuous and luxurious.

That the labor-time (to say nothing of natural values) required for the sumptuous and pernicious products and services, consumed by the appropriators, when compared with their small quantity, was enormous. Their total valuation at the current money prices amounted to nearly *three-fourths* of the whole estimated value of the labor product of the country; the capital invested in lands, buildings, machines, and materials to make them, was *two-thirds* of the assessed value of all property; and the labor they required took more than *one-half* of all the wage people, without counting the officials and soldiers.

That the creepers, soldiers, and officials made *one-fourth* of the wage people, and the fructifyers another fourth. That *this last-named* FOURTH produced the whole quantity of every commodity, and rendered every service usefully consumed by the wage people, who composed *three-fourths* of the whole population. Hence it was calculated that, if all the able-bodied men in the country labored to supply only that which was truly necessary and commodious, it would require only half time to furnish it in the greatest abundance.

Finally, it was remarked that the products, the capital, the merchandise, and indeed all valuable things in the country, could be distinguished as belonging to one or the other of *two* clearly marked destinations; (1) those that were only available to the appropriators, and (2) those that were only fit for the wage people.

But, all these developments did not touch the heart of Enos, and induce him to make more equitable laws. On the contrary, he sought only to strengthen and perpetuate the class distinctions, the monopolies, and the other privileges enjoyed by the few to the detriment of the many. He resolved to rest his throne upon this system. He hastened to create his projected aristocracy; and for this he

14

chose the very richest of the money lords and gentry. He gave them the titles of Prince, Duke, Count, and the like, decorated them with distinctive insignia, and endowed them with peculiar powers and immunities; but, subjected them to many conditions and duties for the maintenance of his royalty and dynasty.

One of the statutes of this aristocracy was, that it should be composed only of those whose wealth was very great and clear of encumbrance. Elevation to higher rank, title, and power was to be the reward of increase of wealth, and divestiture and degradation, the immediate penalty of incurring serious debts or losses. Wealth being the foundation on which the nobility rested, such a creature as a poor nobleman was not tolerated in Nodland. Ruined men, if they had been nobles, were severely punished whenever they attempted to use, or even boast of, their former distinctions and titles.

At the same time, Enos also determined on the conquest and subjugation of the Eden of Labor. For this purpose he raised, armed, and trained a larger standing army than had ever been seen in the world before. He found this even easier than he expected; for the number of the unemployed poor was so great, that hundreds of thousands flocked to the service which secured them even a scanty and perilous existence.

This accomplished, he invaded the Eden of Labor, and thoroughly succeeded in subjecting it to his sovereignty and institutions.

The Patriarchs were deprived of all temporal authority, and forced to fly to the sterile mountains and deserts.

It does not enter into the plan of this work to relate in detail, the means and circumstances of the violent substitution of the institutions of cupidity and envy, to those of equity and brotherhood. Suffice it to say that all the lands and other property of the Reductionese were confiscated and divided among an aristocracy composed of officers of the conquering army, who were rewarded with dignities and booty in proportion to their rank, while the conquered people were reduced to a serfdom similar to that of the feudal system established in Europe by Clovis and Theodoric.

All the aristocracies that ever existed on the face of the earth, whatever name they have borne, were really of wealth. The moment any of them seemingly resting on military distinction or family right, became poor, it fell into contempt and impotency. Enos simply made this practical fact ostensible. He knew that titles of nobility were useless and ridiculous without riches; and that, with riches, there was social elevation and influence that could, were it not for vanity, dispense with honorary names and escutcheons.

CHAPTER X.

DEGRADATION AND REACTION.

Of course, the reader perceives that the institutions of Nodland, and the events of its history, the wrongs and wars, the tyranny and miseries that befell the people of that country, were the natural—nay, the necessary—consequences of the principle of cupidity and appropriation that prevailed there. It could produce no other result. Let us pursue the narrative.

Irad, the confounder of descents and races, succeeded his father Enos, who died about the year 1040. Irad, during his reign, which lasted one hundred and twenty-five years, adopted the policy of encouraging marriages between the victorious and enriched families of Nodland and the ruined, but once distinguished, families of the Eden of Labor. His object was to reconcile the Reductionese to the institutions and order of things Enos had introduced among them. He thought, that, if he afforded their men opportunities of acquiring exceptional riches, he would tempt them to accept the manners and customs according to which such opportunities were presented, and such riches secured. His plan was destined to be ultimately successful. At first only a few of the race of Seth were induced to intermarry with the descendants of Cain; but when the enslaved people saw the parties and children of these alliances aggrandized and enriched, the cupidity of their souls was moved; and gradually more and more of them yielded to the allurement. A door was opened through which, it seemed to every poor slave, he might escape the distress and oppression he suffered. The selfish—the ambitious and covetous—feelings of each individual were stimulated. Each imagined he might be the fortunate suitor of one of the "daughters of men." The hearts of thousands of the once disinterested and fraternal Reductionese were now leavened with avaricious and inequitable hopes and desires. The greed of riches took possession of souls which formerly glowed with neighborly love, so that, as time went on, a majority was converted to the principles of their rapacious conquerors.

Only one dissenting class of men prevented this sentiment from becoming quickly unanimous. It was that of the priesthood, founded by Enoch, the son of Seth, born in the year 235. It was the vocation of the priesthood to offer the daily sacrifice to the only God, and to preserve and teach the traditions of His law. This order still existed in the reign of Enos; and continued zealously for centuries after to fulfil their holy functions. They preached against the growing corruption, and thus greatly retarded its progress. To defeat it entirely was impossible, on account of the abolition of the social and economic system their principles implied. They taught brotherly unity, but the tribes had been forcibly disorganized, families dispersed, and the faithful were the slaves of cruel and insatiate strangers. Each of them was robbed of the fruits of his labor, reduced to the smallest living measure; and this was all they could share with one another. Mutual assistance in labor or suffering was almost impossible; and from among themselves sprang shameless betrayers. But since the political and social organization of the law of love was rendered impossible, the priests advised the disinherited poor to form among themselves associations for mutual help, benevolent societies, unions, and guilds under divine protection. These were voluntarily constituted on various plans. From the beginning they were fruitful of benefits to the members; but, what was more important, they served to prepare the slaves for the emancipation which

14*

followed the civil wars that broke out in different parts of Irad's empire.

The nobility had frequent quarrels with each other, arising sometimes from personal insults, sometimes from an heiress eloping with the younger son of a neighbor, sometimes from depredations of the vassals of others, and sometimes from one nobleman harboring the fugitive slaves of the others. Irad had the weakness to allow the nobles to make war on each other. He regarded it as of no consequence so long as they were dutiful in their allegiance to him, and ready to suspend their dissentions in order, if necessary, to defend his sovereign authority. In fact, their conflicts amused him; and he let them go on till they became so common that petty intestine war was the habitual state of the country. All disputes between the great were settled in that way; and such was the proud, jealous, and vindictive character of these nobles, that these disputes and consequent appeals to arms were of constant occurrence. To meet the exigencies, the nobles would often compose small armies of their slaves; and, to inspire these slaves with ardor, would promise them immunities, such as to commute their slavery for a stipulated tribute of small amount, or for a lease of land on shares of product, or for a percentage on the earnings of co-operative companies, which the workmen were allowed to form. In the mean time, the priests, while seeking by all means to induce the nobles to cease war and live in peace, encouraged—nay even suggested almost every concession made in favor of the servile classes. They denounced the enslavement of persons as a sin, and wherever they persuaded the heart of a nobleman to submit to divine law, they induced him to celebrate his conversion by an act of manumission. Unfortunately, this was not as general as it ought to have been; but it was remarked that trade unions of freedmen gradually augmented; and that, in some parts, they comprised whole towns or communes, which prospered under charters of emancipation wrung by necessity, or obtained through religion, from their former masters.

In the midst of all this, after a reign of one hundred and twenty-five years, Irad died, and his son ascended the throne.

MAJUJAEL, the smitten of God, son of Irad, began his reign about the year 1165. His first act of sovereignty was to forbid the noblemen from granting any further immunities to their menials and bondmen. He prohibited any future liberation of slaves. He forbade the noblemen from making war against each other, ordered them to disband their military retainers, and required them to refer all their disputes to him as their rightful arbitrator. He commanded all the free towns and communes to attorn to him, took away the charters the noblemen had given, and issued new ones with restricted conditions under the great seal of State. A cry of indignation at these measures arose from all classes, and revolt was attempted, but there was no concert of action among the discontents. Majujael sent disciplined armies to all the provinces; and suppressed all signs of rebellion, inflicting the most cruel punishments on every man whose conduct or lukewarmness afforded the least ground to accuse him of disloyalty. Thousands were tortured and burned to death. Great estates were forfeited to the crown; and given away to abject courtiers.

But far from consolidating his sovereignty by this violent and sudden change of the policy of the State, or by this undue severity, a contrary affect was in a short time developed. Many of the patriarchs and their families had taken refuge in the mountainous districts when Irad subjugated the Eden of Labor. There they had lived in peace, leading a pastoral life. Enoch, son of Seth, and Cainan, son of Enoch, had presided over their restricted but undisturbed territory and fraternal society. To the same mountains great numbers of the people now fled to escape Majujael's persecution. Mahlaleel, now the ruling patri-

arch (for Enoch and Cainan were dead) was greatly
embarrassed to relieve the wants of such a multitude
of refugees. It was at once manifest that he could
not support them long, whatever generous sacrifices
he and his people were disposed to make. Their
account of the barbarity of Majujael fired his heart
with indignation, but what could he do to succor them
effectually? Suddenly he was "illumined of God."
He observed that, as if inspired by a common thought,
they had come to him for protection; and without
pre-concert were here and now, as it were, an army
of more than an hundred thousand men providen-
tially assembled and only needing organization and a
leader.

Without hesitation Mahlaleel availed himself of
the situation, procured arms and provisions, mar-
shalled the fugitives, recruited reinforcements among
the herdsmen of the mountains, marched against the
tyrant, overthrew him in a great battle: and as
Supreme Patriarch took upon himself the government
of the country where Adam had reigned with so much
beneficence and wisdom.

He exerted all his genius to re-establish the laws
and customs of the Eden of Labor; but met with
unexpected difficulties. The people had become corrupted by the principles of the Appropriative System. They clamored for it in the name of Liberty.
They understood as liberty the right of getting rich
under the protection of uncharitable laws that guaranteed to every man whatsoever he could gain from the
making of inequitable and uncharitable bargains with
his neighbors, or by the privileged appropriation of
natural values, etc. The hope even the poorest
entertained of winning a prize in this iniquitous lot-
tery, where nearly all the chances were held by capital against labor, blinded them to their true interests.

Nevertheless, after proclaiming the emancipation
of the slaves, he persisted in his efforts to restore
Reductionism, and was making considerable though

prudently graduated progress, when he found himself
obliged to engage in another war.

MATHUSAEL, the death dealer, son of Majujael, had
in the year 1195, succeeded his father as king of Nodland; and raised a new army to conquer the Eden of
Labor again. He marched against Mahlaleel, van-
quished and slew him. Not content with simple vic-
tory, he followed up his success by a general massacre
of those who had yielded even a semblance of allegiance to Mahlaleel's government. Blood flowed in
torrents over the whole land. The people were deci-
mated, but, strange to say, they did not murmur; they
only wept their friends and relatives; for with all his
barbarity, Mathusael cunningly managed to console
them. He confirmed or rather imitated Mahlaleel's
edict of emancipation, disturbed no inheritance, and
proclaimed what he called free trade, but which could
be only defined as a license to all men (particularly
those who had managed to appropriate to self an
amount of natural values) to accumulate additional
wealth through profit, rent, and usury which they
deducted from the fruits of labor. Yet this was what
the great majority desired and applauded, so that, notwithstanding his blood-thirsty ferocity, Mathusael was
popular and enjoyed a peaceful reign.

LAMECH, conquerer of the poor, son of Mathusael
became in 1260 the worthy successor of his father
as *ruler* of the nations. In the first part of his
reign nothing occurred to disturb the settled policy
and economic movement of the empire; but after
some years a double evolution manifested itself.
The aristocracy founded, as we have seen, on wealth
claimed the right of taking part in the government and demanded a parliament, the wagemen
began to realize the fact of the utter hopelessness
of any amelioration of their condition from any
voluntary or initial movement on the part of their
masters the appropriators. The wealthy argued
that since they supported the State; were taxed to
pay all expenses of administration, the cost of civil

police and warlike defence, with armies, navies, and
munitions, guards, detectives, constables, and judges,
and were required generally to provide all the revenues needed for public works and public justice,
they should be consulted and their consent obtained.
They contended for the principle of no taxation
without representation. The poor argued that true
it was there should be no taxation without representation; but that all the taxes were in fact paid by
them—paid from the proceeds of their labor, and
hence the law and national institutions and economy
should have due regard to their welfare. They were
willing even to support the king should he refuse
the representation the wealthy demanded; but
Lamech was well aware that the whole fabric of the
Nodlandic constitution was built upon the supremacy
of the wealthy; and upon the design of securing
quiet to the ownerships and appropriations acquired
according to the intensely selfish legislation of Cain.
He therefore cheerfully called the parliament required
by the NOBILITY, and by the COMMONERS *who were
property holders*, but treated the timid petition of the
wagemen with utter contempt. To this parliament,
which was composed of two houses, a senate of titled
grandees, and a delegation of rich commoners, the
wagemen appealed to obtain relief from many of the
hardships their masters imposed; but it was a vain
attempt; for it was really asking the appropriators
to decide their own case against themselves.

Thus repelled, the wagemen fell back upon their
unions, and inaugurated *strikes;* also tried to form
co-operative associations to do work on their own
account: but in both these movements they met with
the most effectual opposition. The appropriators
answered the strikes by lock-outs and combined
inertia; the co-operative enterprises by refusing the
necessary funds except for usury, thus rendering the
co-operation just as tributary to them as any other
individual or partnership undertaking based on borrowed capital, or they would combine to undersell

the co-operatives till they exhausted and ruined them. Nevertheless these unions and strikes were troublesome; and the appropriators resolved to get rid of them by means of invidious and punitory laws, which were passed in the two houses, and which received the royal sanction, defining the strikes as riotous assemblies and the unions as conspiracies, and prohibiting as criminal any attempt to enlist, or to shame, or deter, such workmen as were willing to accept whatever wages the employers chose to give.

These laws were rigorously enforced, so that by the time of Lamech's death the wagemen were completely reduced to subjection.

In the mean time, however, political events arose which it is useless to explain, but which induced Lamech to think it good policy to strengthen for a while the voluntary unions the laboring people had formed. He granted them charters, with power to pass *regulations* obligatory, AS LAW, upon every member. These charters decreed that *all* the workers of the same trade should belong to the corporate body of his craft—that each union might own property and undertake works, in its corporate capacity—determine at what wages and during what number of hours per day it would be lawful for a member to work—and to refuse to allow a member to leave the union in which he had voluntarily enrolled himself.

Soon, under these sanctions, the working class rose to prosperity, and even to power. Hence they loved—were faithful to and proud of their organization. But Lamech, covetous of the property they had acquired, seeking means to indulge the unbounded luxury and pomp of his court, and to levy men and materials for building wonderful, but useless, palaces and monuments, burdened the unions with enormous taxes and onerous services to the State; this to an extent the unions could not sustain. They were crushed under the load imposed by the arbitrary edicts of the empire; and the members fell into a worse slavery and poverty than before.

JABAL, JUBAL, and TUBALCAIN, the worldly pro-ducers and possessors, sons of Lamech, were, about the year 1360, severally called to rule over different parts of the empire of the world. Their father had had four sons, two by each of his wives Ada and Sella. He held them in equal affection; and, seeing that his empire was so large, conceived the idea of dividing his succession among them, which he did by means of a will of which he left a copy with each of them, to be opened only at the moment of his death. One day, however, for some slight offence, he flew into a passion against the second son of Ada, and slew him. His sorrow for this was so great that he never recollected himself sufficiently to think of correcting the dispositions of the will. Upon its being opened, it threw, as it were, the apple of dis-cord among the lords, commons, and people. How was the portion bequeathed to the murdered son to be disposed of or divided? Should the empire be divided at all? These were questions which aroused the ambition and the jealousies of different parties. Factions, each demanding a discordant solution, were formed; and in a few weeks the world was ablaze with civil war. It followed, after many years of bloodshed and devastation, that, instead of three or four kingdoms, double as many arose, and several oligarchies and republics were constituted.

The result of this revolution, so far as the wage-men were concerned, was only this, that they ac-quired everywhere the right of suffrage, but how to exercise it wisely, and to their own and the gene-ral welfare, they failed to perceive. Demagogues went among them advocating the pursuit of many good objects, such as: the reduction of the hours of labor; education; the lending of capital to the poor that they might become independent producers; the taxation of each man's gross capital, whether in debts due him or otherwise, and without regard to his net

fortune; the encouragement of co-operative enterprises by the State; the division of lands into small
farms; the abolition of usury, and the like; but none
of the reformers were able to point out *how* these
reforms were to be effected, either through violence
or peaceful means. They kept the world in constant
agitation and apprehension, without there being any
reasonable prospect of a happy change. The practical objections to their plans seemed insuperable.
Education must be a mockery so long as the children of the poor must be set to work, at ten years of
age, to avoid dying of starvation and cold. A diminution of the hours of labor must be vain so long as
the rate of wages and the number of wagemen employed depended upon the will or ability of the
employers. Strikes for higher wages in any trade
could be efficient only in the few cases where the
profits of the masters afforded margin for compli-
ance; but in every other instance higher wages could
only ruin the masters and therefore the workmen
also. Co-operation only instituted partnerships
composed of numerous members, but subject to all
the accidents and losses of similar enterprises con-
ducted by single persons or corporations. The par-
cellation of land must be ineffective so long as it may
be sold in perpetuity, and reconsolidated after division, and so long as the hiring of agricultural wagemen was permitted. Usury could not be prevented
by any imaginable legislation, so long as accumulation of capital by one man and the need of it by
another is lawfully possible, and so long as rent,
profit, and credit can be legally stipulated between
contracting parties. Taxation imposed in an unequal
or excessive manner, for the purpose of compelling
the few who had accumulated the capital of a country
to distribute it among the many, was not only con-
fiscation, to the detriment of those who had at least
a semblance of title in order to pass that title to
others who could show no claim whatever; but such
a mere change of title was an admission of the very

15

property principle which it only served to complicate and embarrass, and was certain to bring on sudden ruin to all, without certainty of benefit to any.

Though obviously impracticable, the mere proposing of these measures terrified and angered the appropriators. They saw ruin to themselves in any legislative attempt, however short-lived, to realize them, so they bethought themselves of every way in which the people might be deterred from electing the would be reformers who proposed them. Of course they diligently refuted them through their orators and their presses. In doing this they enjoyed the greatest advantage; for the most eloquent speakers, the best writers, and the greatest publishers were at their service. Capital alone could furnish the patronage, the custom, and the readers. Capital could alone offer the reward or bribe which the speakers and writers coveted, and could alone print great quantities of papers and books.

This did not, however, quiet the solicitude of the appropriators. They sought and found other means of turning the current of the universal desire for a better organization of society into useless reservoirs and deceitful eddies. They excited the people to take sides in regard to questions which might be decided in one way or the other without bringing about any change in the condition of the wagemen: questions which only concerned the interests of the appropriators in their rivalries of each other, or which were only idly speculative, or which might corrupt public morals without destroying chances of gain or ambition. Among these were questions of war and peace between nations; tariffs or free trade; the creation or destruction of monopolies; the proper imposition and standard of taxes; internal improvements, whether expedient here or there or at all; the good or bad administration of public revenues; the corruption or virtues of particular aspirants for popular favor; paper-money and banks, whether they should be al-

lowed or not, and, if at all, to what extent and in
what form; sectional interests—the interest of a district
or locality treated as beneficial to every inhabitant
when only its appropriators were concerned; State
encouragement of one religion and its persecution of
another; women's rights; free love; and so forth.

On these and a hundred other *false issues* parties
were formed, and the nations kept in a state of continual revolution, while the appropriators watched
every change to make speculations and derive gain.
They were, as a body, indifferent of the success of
any party or cause, provided they could foresee it,
and make money by it. They advocated the party
on whose chances of success they had staked investments, just as a sportsman bets on and praises the
horse he thinks will win, though he has no real affection for the animal. They cared little what form of
government existed. They only dreaded a change
that might, in any way (1) deprive them of gain from
natural values, (2) modify the ownership of land so
that they could not derive rent from it forever, or (3)
prevent them from taking for themselves any part of
the fruits of the labors of other men.

Whether they intended it or not, this agitation of
every vain question, and the supremacy universally
conceded to the principles of the selfish system of
political economy; the possibilities and opportunities
this system presented for the accumulation of exceptional wealth, and the consequent enjoyment of exceptional sumptuousness and pleasure, corrupted
almost every heart; tempted those who might hope
to gratify their passions, and made those who could
not have even the hope of justice, doubt the possibility of virtue. Even the Patriarch Mathusalech
joined the spoilers of labor, and revelled in every
sensual excess. The common people gave themselves
to drunkenness and the other brutal vices. The
lords and gentry were no better, only they veiled
their corruption under appearances of polite refine-
ment; but their excesses were really more debasing,

and proved a less regard for divine commandments, than those of the rest of mankind.

Nevertheless, it was an age of science and invention: an age of material progress. Jabal, Jubal, and Tubalcain were themselves great inventors. Tubalcain was not only deeply versed in mechanics, but also in the arts of war. It was he whom the Greeks afterwards adored as Vulcan, or as Mars. His sister, Naomah, the beauteous, was remembered and worshipped as Venus. On their palaces and cities, and on their persons and living, they lavished millions. They sought to evince the beautiful and the sublime in all things material. They cultivated art for its own sake, and without regard to the true and the good. They brought music, sculpture, and painting to the highest sensual perfection. They built great monuments, erected wonderful machinery, paved roads, dug canals; but above all things, invented and manufactured fearfully destructive arms, which *the State only* could command and possess in considerable quantity; and which the men in power put into the hands of their numerous and subservient soldiers, to keep the degraded people in complete subjection.

CHAPTER XI.

THE DELUGE OF SIN AND DEATH.

ONE family only remained faithful to God : it was that of NOAH, who was, therefore, reserved " to give us comfort from the works and labors of our hands on the earth which the Lord had cursed." (Gen. v. 29.) Born after the conquest of the Eden of Labor by Enos, and when the Reductionese had become to a great extent corrupted, the grace was given him to receive his early education from those who had preserved and imbibed the traditions of the early patriarchs, and particularly from those who continued the teachings of Enoch, son of Jared, he of whom the Scripture says: " he walked with God; and was seen no more, because God had taken him." So, also, Noah "was a just and perfect man in his generations; he walked with God." (Gen. vi. 9.) During the reign of Lamech, and of the three sons of Lamech, Noah, inspired of God, sought to recall men from their iniquities, and to persuade them to resume *voluntarily* the brotherly exchange of labor for labor, which the Reductionese formerly practised. Noah understood the vanity of any attempt at material reform by any of the measures the politicians and economists were trying or proposing. Hence, he reminded the ancients, and endeavored to inform the young, of the system based upon the clear distinction between God's share and man's share of all products, and on the gratuitousness of natural values, and the consequent limitation of price to labor value only. He described the beautiful prosperity which had prevailed while this principle was acted on; but at the same time, knowing that *the principle rested on religious conviction*, and could be successfully applied only by those who believed it was the will of God

15*

and would obey it as such, he sought principally to
rebuke infidelity and restore the true faith. Strange
to say, that, though men were living who knew Adam
and Eve themselves, there were great numbers of
people who treated the history of creation and of
Eden as dreams of deluded dotards or inventions
of impostors. Even among those who were regarded
in popular opinion as faithful and pious, a large proportion conceived God as a being subject to external
necessity; and, therefore, of limited power and wisdom. Many believed in the eternity of matter; and
in the existence of an Evil Spirit, in every respect
the equal of the Author of all Good. Sorcery, di-
vination, the evocation and worship of demons, idolatry, and a thousand other superstitions had become
common; but, worse than all, a wide-spread spirit of
scepticism treated every point of faith and morals
as an "open question," which every man was left to
decide for himself, as his measure of knowledge and
intellect enabled him, or as his passions dictated.
By a strange inconsistency, however, the noisiest
claimants of liberty of thought and action were
fatalists and materialists who denied man's freedom
of will, declared that his acts were automatic, that
his religion and morality were determined wholly
by birthplace, climate, education, and other ex-
trinsic circumstances. They believed that there was
no Heaven-derived law, and that virtue was merely
a word to which various meanings were attached,
according to the expediency or policy human reason
or popular prejudice adopted in the course of
historical transitions. Hence, in discarding revelation, they considered themselves as subjected to a
coercion entirely accidental and material, a coercion
that exempted them from all moral responsibility,
and authorized them to gratify every animal propensity or passion whenever they could, or thought
they could, do so with impunity. Hence, also,
though they professed a scientific and æsthetical re-
finement, and made dissertations on natural morality,

their theory furnished them with no sure and certain rule of conduct, tended to carry them into habitual vice, and to tempt them to the commission of every crime. Such indeed was the result. "The wickedness of man was great on the earth, and . . . all the thoughts of their hearts were bent on evil at all times." (Gen. vi. 5.)

Before God passed his final sentence, Noah went among men, and threatened them with divine justice if they did not repent and turn to the Lord; but they derided him as a madman, and continued in their impiety, dissoluteness, and crime. Thinking that he might find a few hundred, who might be willing to separate themselves and form a righteous community, which would, by giving an example of brotherhood and piety, excite the admiration of the world and draw it back to justice and to God, he devised a plan for that purpose. He proposed a league, which might be joined by any number of the class of fructifyers, that is to say, those who worked at producing whatsoever was "good for the poor," and within the means of the poor; with a compact between the members that they would exchange their products on the principle of labor-time value for equal labor-time value. He proposed that they should each devotedly contract and sternly perform the obligation *never to exchange a product or service in which an ascertained amount of average labor-time was embodied for a product or service of* LESS *average labor-time value.* This LEAGUE would have differed materially from the co-operative companies and guilds attempted in previous and after ages; for, it was not to consist of men of a single trade, but of *all* trades doing work of the NECESSARY kind, such as raising provisions, building plain dwellings, making substantial articles, providing fuel, besides constructing and running machinery and vehicles, or manufacturing and using tools and implements *necessary for such work.* He argued with them that if they did this, in a spirit of self-sacrifice and indomitable perseverance, they would free themselves from the extortion of the appropriators of all classes. He showed them that indefinite extension could be given to such a measure; and that all the wagemen, and even the appropriators, might successively adopt it, so that mankind in general could be at last embraced in its operation, on this condition only, that, for the time being, they would cease the production of extravagant and costly articles, and devote their labor only to what was really necessary and good for themselves and the rest of the poor. He said their labor should produce that which each one from his own labor might purchase and live by; and that if a " LEAGUE OF VARIOUS NECESSARY TRADES" were formed to work and exchange on this principle, it would procure its members abundance of everything proper to use and consume; besides, at the same time, obtaining for every one of them abundance of rest.

He showed them that such a result could not be effected from the simple co-operation of workmen of the *same trade*. That a simple union of persons of a particular art, working together to produce a special commodity, then seeking to derive the highest price, and dividing the proceeds among themselves, only isolated the co-operators from the rest of the poor, made their interests distinct and adverse, even to those of associations of other trades, which worked on the same plan of detached unions or partnerships. That the members of the same trade could not exchange their products with one another, and, therefore, that each of their associations stood in the same relation to the rest of the world as ordinary individuals did, would be tempted by the same selfish motives, would act as all independent corporations do—aim at monopoly and separate accumulation. The members of the shoemaker's unions, for instance, could not exchange their goods with one another; the hatters could not exchange with one another; but exchanges are necessarily made between shoemakers and hatters. He showed them that the same objection was also applicable to *close* communes or associations of co-operative labor, *even though they embraced* SEVERAL *trades;* and that if exchanges are made between separate associations on the selfish principle, at money prices determined by the caprice of desire, or the speculations of competition, or the greed of monopoly, there would be no real change, but only a nominal displacement of private persons, and a substitution of corporations acting from the same motives, and in the same manner as before—seeking to extract the utmost profit from each other. Clearly *a complex association of many trades*, agreeing to exchange work and products, by labor value only, would remove conflicting interests, and permit the benefits of universal brotherhood to be realized. It would defeat all the machinations of the appropriators.

He suggested their primary attempts should be to form such a complex association of trades as would form a *complete circuit* and conveyance of exchanges, though it might be on the smallest practical and economical sale. For this he enumerated the following elements as necessary: (1) LAND, having cultivated fields, cattle, woods, water-power, clay, sand, and stone; (2) a COAL MINE; (3) an IRON MINE; (4) a MANUFACTORY of utensils, findings, tools, and implements; (5) a FOUNDERY and forge for constructing engines; (6) a SAW MILL, with carpenter, cabinet-maker, blacksmith, and wheelwright *shops;* (7) a cloth and clothing FACTORY, for making only such textile fabrics as are indispensable; (8) a TANNERY, with currier and shoemaker's shop, soap and tallow-maker's vats; (9) a FLOURING and GRIST MILL; (10) a KILN, for burning brick and lime, with brickmaker's and bricklayer's appurtenances; and (11) a TYPE FOUNDERY, paper mill, and printing office. All these he calculated could be supported in certain efficient and economical proportions, by a population of ten thousand mechanics and agriculturists adequately apportioned, so that no person's time would be wasted, and so as to supply one another with all things necessary and commodious in profusion.

Noah even promised them riches if they followed this counsel; and to prove the possibility of attaining riches by this means, he propounded what seemed a *paradox*, but was indeed a demonstration, as follows:—

If everybody were poor, all would have to work; there would be no idleness.

If none were idle and all were poor, everybody would have to *work for the poor;* there would be nobody else to work for.

If there were none to work for but the poor, and none were idle, the poor would be working for one another, and they would only do or make things *good for the poor*.

If all worked to make only such things as are good for the poor, there would be abundance of such things.

If the poor had abundance of all things good for them, they would not be poor, but rich; for abundance is riches.

Hence the true paradox: *if all were poor, all would be rich*.

Its truth will appear clearly to the mind by remembering the Eden of Labor where everybody worked at necessary and cheap yet commodious and beautiful production, and nobody worked at sham, dead, or wicked production; and where none could make profit on the work of others; and where it was impossible for individuals to accumulate exceptional riches. In that country there were no thieves, for its economic order gave little or no temptation to steal; there were no envyings, for no cause for them could arise. Hence, too, in that country, there was never occasion for lawsuits or quarrels for property; and no need of sheriffs, or seizures, or the like. The intrinsic and self acting operations of its laws were such that within its borders there were no monopolies, no capitalists, no usurers, no hirers, no landlords,

no speculators, no drones, no luxurious living, no
aristocracy of riches, no sumptuous fashions, no gew-
gaws, no frippery, no life of vanity and frivolity.
Its people did not eat if they did not work. They
lived in brotherhood—were necessarily temperate—
produced and enjoyed all things in mutuality and
equity—enjoyed healthful rest and intellectual leisure—worshipped and obeyed God, in truth and in
love.

Hence the true paradox: *If none were allowed to
get richer than his brethren, all would be rich.*

But all the efforts of Noah were vain, all his arguments fell upon hearts and minds hermetically closed.

So corrupted had their souls become, that they
would not believe in his honesty, truthfulness, or
disinterestedness; and imagined he was actuated by
some secret design of ambition or cupidity.

Sometimes he would say to them: "If you think
it will take too long to restore the Eden of Labor to
its plenitude and perfection, why do you not attempt
reforms which, though only partial and empirical,
would have a tendency to that end? For instance,
you might do this. Have an account taken to ascertain the average *necessary* annual expense of a work-
ingman's family—the food, the clothes, the fuel, the
rent, the literature, the medicine which a poor family
composed of husband, wife, and two children cannot
dispense with without suffering. Say this would
amount to eight hundred ounces of silver per annum.
Divide this by two hundred, and let the dividend be
the lawful *minimum* price of one day's work—the
labor time being eight hours. A day's wage would
therefore be four ounces of silver—an hour's wage
half an ounce. But let this dividend vary with the
rise and fall of the total price-current of things included in the account. For example, suppose the
cost of a year's poor living fell to seven hundred
ounces, the wage would be $3\frac{50}{100}$ ounces. If the cost
of living rose to nine hundred ounces, the day's wage
would be $4\frac{50}{100}$. Have an inexorable law declaring

that this *minimum* thus ascertained shall be paid for
the fair amount of work an average toiler can do,
excess over the average to be paid at the same rate,
per hour or per day. Thus an *equilibrium* between
the cost of living and the price of labor would be
maintained. A margin would be left for the appropriators to prey *upon each other*, through speculations,
demand, and supply, the competition of desire and
free trade, to the full extent of the surplus of necessary products and of all commodious and sumptuous
things ; but a limit would be set to their oppression
of those whose labor and skill produce the riches
they appropriate. The poorest reward of labor would
at least be guaranteed. Perhaps you will object that
many attempts have been made to fix the price of
labor or commodities by means of legislation and
authority—that these attempts have been vain—that
such laws have been always evaded and have always
produced the contrary effect. Yes, but it was because
the law fixed the prices arbitrarily—fixed them according to no principle. The law makers never thought to
rest their tariff only on the primary and necessary consideration of the cost of supporting labor—they have
never thought of the rule that labor must at least
reproduce itself—they have never thought of main-
taining the equilibrium between the cost of support
and the price of labor on the principle and by the
means I suggest. The plates of the scales in which
these two are weighed against each other should all
the time be kept on a perfect level. As soon as the
balance begins to be disturbed, the deficit of the one
should be supplied, or the excedent of the other be re-
moved. Do you insist that such a law might be evaded
by contract and acquittance—by payments in merchandise at excessive prices or by the indirect return of
a part of every payment, or by false acknowledg-
ments of debt, or some other simulation—which the
workman would from necessity be compelled to
acknowledge in writing or before witnesses? I reply :
Enforce honest and real payment by self-operative

laws. Declare that every contract of hire entered into for wages below the lawful rate is contrary to public policy, and therefore void so far as it attempts to evade that standard. Leave the inquiry into the real state of every case always open. Reserve to the hired workman who may have worked for less, the right, at any time afterward (for instance after ceasing to work for an employer) to sue for the difference between what necessity compelled him to accept and the amount which would have been justly due him according to the statute. Provide rules by which the truth may be manifested, and subterfuges detected. Admit all evidence, direct and circumstantial, of advantage taken of the workman's distress, or of his hire having been unfairly withheld. Let his right of action descend to his widow and orphans. Such a law would render futile every attempt to evade it. It would deter the appropriators from even making such attempt; for, they would always fear that after the workman's discharge he would demand justice, or that after his death his widow or orphans might unmask false appearances and inequitable artifices and thereupon would recover what had been fictitiously receipted for or unjustly withheld on colorable grounds. Yes, and it would be well to add that they should be on conviction condemned to pay four-fold. If such a law were passed I think the appropriators would cease from seeking an increase of profit or the avoidance of loss by reducing the price of labor below an adequate living standard. As the rate of wages would be ever and inexorably on a level with his adequate support, the appropriators would look for elements of profit outside of this condition. Perhaps (nay, certainly) they would provide for the production of a greater abundance of necessary things, which thereby would become cheaper, and thus procure a reduction of the money-price of wages without its affecting in the least the amount of things necessary for support which the workman would obtain."

16

Many wagemen thought this was an excellent remedy for the oppressive advantage the appropriators took, on every opportunity, to reduce the rate of wages. The unions in some places adopted it, and proposed to give their votes only to such candidates for office as would pledge themselves to carry it into effect; but, alas! they never could become unanimous in this or anything else. On this and many other plans and purposes they were ever in discord. They differed furiously and enviously on the choice of persons—they harbored jealous and malicious feelings toward each other—quarrelled and fought about every trifling matter—preferred failure and ruin to success and happiness that might be derived from the efforts of any one they disliked—hate instead of love ruled their hearts and actions—they formed coteries whose principal business was to undermine each other while they neglected the common interests of their class—the great majority paid no attention whatever to the questions that concerned the interests of labor—each man pursued only his momentary impulse—transitory advantage—dominant passion or vice. They ran to and fro after the illusory changes proposed by demagogues and financiers—free traders and free lovers—hard and soft money men—liberals and atheists—spirit-raisers and sensational orators. They lived in a chaos of impiety, hate, violence, sensuality, theft, fraud, falsehood, treachery, intemperance, and incontinence. They had lost faith in God and man —lost human sympathy—had become sordidly self ish—scoffed at philanthropy and virtue. Their degradation and inability to act on principles of charity sank lower every day.

During Noah's mission there happened a most extraordinary event which must not be left unmentioned in this book. It was the discovery of prodigiously abundant mines of gold and silver in ten thousand places of the world. In every mountain range eager eyes and hands of searchers detected and unearthed the precious ores in so many places and in such vast quantities that at last they became as common as stone. At first, a mine was discovered on the side of a mountain in an uninhabited territory. Hundreds, as soon as they heard of it and of the riches it afforded the lucky finder, made expeditions to the region, with the hope of similar good fortune. The world was in a fever of excitement awaiting the result. By and by, news came that the success of the pioneers was wonderful: that they had found much more than expected. Then some of them returned bringing great loads of gold dust and virgin silver. On this, the fever immediately rose to frenzy. The hundreds who went first were followed by thousands, and then by tens of thousands who left the labor they were doing in the fields and cities to appropriate the wealth profusely lavished by nature and which was easily and rapidly gathered. Every one of these adventurers secured great heaps of the object of their cupidity. A great many of them established their permanent residence near the mines, and sent their great booty to the cities by every means of conveyance. Others returned home in the vessels and vehicles which carried cargoes of these enormous treasures. All imagined they had gained exceedingly great riches; but lo! they had defeated themselves, for they had such an overwhelming excess of gold and silver to offer in exchange for everything else, that these metals fell in comparative value to almost nothing.

The effect of this may be more easily imagined than described. The currency, the medium of exchange, was ruined at its basis. The common standard by which values were compared was lost. A great weight and volume of it was of small value. Its convenience for circulation was destroyed. The glory of hard money vanished. It had become as rubbish. The term of computation of values, whether called a shekel or talent, ceased to have a meaning   The currency had rested on the scarcity of gold and silver, and the slow increase of their total quantity in the world; but now these conditions no longer existed. Hence all buying and selling or other contracts, by means of it, were impracticable; and commerce was deranged and retarded —nearly broken up. Rich men whose fortunes amounted to millions in stocks, bonds, notes, coin and the like, now saw these things, recently so valuable, had ceased to be so. Thousands of the wealthy were thus suddenly reduced to poverty.

The most notable features of this crisis were (1) that the great commercial world (Babylon) found itself all at once without a circulating medium or even a basis for paper money; (2) that it was necessary to find a substitute for the former coins and for the paper that promised them; and (3) that it was necessary to invent a currency that had no reference whatever to any metallic unit.

The world was confounded. The fable of Midas was now realized to almost every man. Gold and silver (now depreciated almost one hundred per centum) were tendered at their denominational standards to the creditor who demanded his due; and he turned away with disgust from the proffered payment, for he already possessed more of the glittering materials than he could apply to any adequate use. The debtor, at the same time, had much more than enough to pay all he owed, but could buy hardly anything with the surplus. Every body was enraged. Quarrels and litigation arose on the obligation and performance of all previous contracts. The governments themselves insisted on paying their enormous national debts in the gold coin they had promised and which their enraged creditors were forced to take according to the figure of the weight printed on their bonds, though it represented a wonderfully less value than it did when the bonds were issued. Thus, having cynically cleared themselves of their debts, the governments breathed again, and rejoiced in the prospect of creating new debts as monstrous as the first. Producers and mer-

chants who had stores of provisions and other commodities refused to sell for lawful money. Workshops and factories were suspended and stores closed.
Vessels and carriages lay most of the time idle.
Great numbers of wagemen were thrown out of
employ just at the moment when the savings made by
painful privations during years of hard labor, lost
nearly all their purchasing value. The proprietors of
commodities concealed their stocks for fear the government would compel them to sell for money at fixed
prices, or that the famishing people would forcibly
despoil them. It was vain to attempt to preserve
peace in the midst of this derangement and obstruc-
tion of trade, labor, and production. The universal
distress drove men to desperation. Mobs, proscription,
pillage, and bloodshed took place everywhere and on
occasion of all manner of alarming rumors. Panics
broke out and spread in every direction. Almost
every act of the government was opposed by riot and
revolt.

In the mean time, however, the ruin of gold and
silver, as currency or basis of currency, became a settled and conceded fact. Hence these metals were
applied to new uses. Being cheaper than iron, glass,
porcelain, or mahogany, and at the same time more
beautiful, they were used to make articles of furniture such as bureaus, desks, bookcases, tables, bed-
steads, stoves, kitchen utensils, and even railings of
balconies and public squares. Indeed gold was preferred to iron in all instances in which iron had formerly served to make things which had to be exposed
to the weather; for it was less liable to corrosion,
substantial enough, and did not cost as much.

But I need not attempt to describe the revulsion
and disorder more particularly. The reader can
readily picture to himself what would be his situation, that of the people in general, and that of the
country and its affairs if all the coin and paper-money
in his own hands and in the hands of all other men
in the world were suddenly so much reduced in value

16*

as to need to be increased ten thousand times in bulk, in order to represent an equal value; and this too when no substitute had been provided.

There was, however, an effect that might not be thought of by every reader. This crisis did not ruin every body, but it increased the *comparative* riches of those who possessed lands, houses, materials, hardware, dry goods, fuel, provisions, and other property in considerable quantity. The moneyed men and those who depended on their prosperity were the only ones who were *directly* struck by the event. Those who possessed any valuable things except money were relatively enriched.

In the midst of the turmoil and hardships of the crisis, the people had recourse to the primitive method of barter, whenever it was practicable to do so, but the cases were few and difficult. Something more effectual and general was absolutely necessary. Rapine by stealth and violence were daily becoming more prevalent. The people must perish unless the regular round of (1) Labor, (2) Production, (3) Exchange, (4) Commerce, (5) Distribution, (6) Consumption, (7) Demand and Labor, and Reproduction again were resumed. The popular voice spontaneously called for a new and safe currency as the only means of restoring peace and prosperity. Thus, every mind was intent upon finding a convenient, light, and quick medium of exchange, based upon an irrefragable and universal unit of value, and excluding gold and silver, which were no longer fit for that purpose.

In some places individuals or corporations tried to supply this desideratum by issuing their personal notes, some promising to do an hour or a day's labor for a definite quantity of a commodity or service they needed, and considered equivalent; or others would make notes promising a measure or weight of one commodity for a certain weight or measure of another; but as every bargain requires at least two persons to make it, several minds and wants had to

concur on the exact quantity of the two elements
mentioned in the note as then respectively needed
by the parties, and as being of equal value. Hence,
with respect to every note it was necessary to find
somebody ready and willing to deliver the precise
thing demanded by the drawer of the note on the
terms proposed, and also willing to rely on the drawer's promise to redeem, by furnishing, on demand, at
any future time the precise service or thing proffered
in exchange. Indeed, these notes amounted simply
to the *tender*, in each, of a specific contract of barter
on credit put into the form of a note, transferable by
delivery. If any one did not need to make that particular bargain, he would most probably refuse the
note; but if, nevertheless, he gave his goods or work
for it, he ran the risk of not finding any one willing
to give him anything for it; besides the risk of the
accidents which might happen to the maker; and also
that of the maker's imprudent proneness to promise
more than he could fulfil; or, indeed, the risk of a
dishonest repudiation of the obligation.

The attempt to give circulation to such notes as a
substitute for money was therefore a failure.

Manifestly the government and the law, whether
local or general, were alone competent to furnish the
desired medium of exchange. (There was, indeed, a
way for private enterprise to do so, but this was not
perceived.) The princes and legislature were, therefore, clamorously called upon to undertake the task,
and they were not slow in responding to the demand.
The expedient most generally adopted was this: The
government (1) imposed *a tax* PAYABLE IN KIND; and
(2) instituted an *assize of equivalents* for its payment.
This assize was based on a *unit of assessment* called
THE ACE, which was determined by declaring (according to the best results of a careful and searching
comparison of former and recent *market prices*) what
quantity and quality of each article should be taken
as equal. For example:—

Eight lbs. ordinary cotton	One ace.
Six lbs. fair cotton	"
250 lbs. gold	"
500 lbs. silver	"
Two barrels bituminous coal	"
One barrel and a half light or cannel coal . .	"
Five dozen eggs	"
Six and a quarter lbs. prime sugar . . .	"
Six and an eighth lbs. choice sugar . . .	"
Three yards No. 1 bolt linen (48 threads to inch)	"
Three-fourths of a yard No. 15 bolt linen (128 threads to inch)	"
2000 *ems* type-setting and distribution . .	"

and so on through all *classifiable* articles known to commerce, or services needed by the government.

In advance of the collection of the assize tax the State issued notes of different decimal denominations; the lowest was for the hundredth of an ace; the highest was for one thousand aces.

In assessing the tax, the government valued all property in aces, and fixed the levy at so much per centum or per mill in aces, leaving it optional with the owners of the property taxed, to pay in the assize notes or in any commodity mentioned in the schedule of equivalents.

If any one paid his tax in kind, the things he delivered were used by the government if it needed them for any purpose. If it did not need them they were sold at auction for aces; but taxes were rarely paid in kind; for, as soon as the tax on any commodity was paid in kind, the assize on it was raised by proclamation to a stricter equation, so that the State might not lose by the sale at auction.

As long as the government did not issue an excessive quantity of its notes, viz., not more than three times the annual revenue, this paper fulfilled all the purposes and duties of the former currency very well.

Nor did this system interfere with the incurring of a new national debt to pay expenses of wars, etc. Whenever the government wanted to borrow, it issued bonds payable in aces, and bearing interest payable in aces. At the same time, it raised the rate of taxation to pay the interest, and a certain portion of the capital annually, also payable in aces. Those who directly or indirectly furnished the government with arms, ammunition, and other things, those who had accumulated aces and wanted to invest them safely at interest, or who speculated on the fluctuation of "the funds," would eagerly subscribe to the required loan.

A metal basis for this operation was wholly unnecessary. The assize-tax, *the right of the government to take the property of the people*, and hand it over in kind to pay the capital and interest due the bond-holders, was a guaranty entirely adequate to a promise of coin, in times when coin was valuable.

In determining the equivalents, this assize-money-system ignored the embodied average labor-time—provided no way of computing it—did not recognize it the only constituent of value—did not distinguish it from natural value or the value of desire—confounded and disregarded every element of value, to look only to the *current market price*, whatever it might be from the influences of free competition or successful appropriation.

Noah thought this great money crisis would cause the nations to discern the error of their financial laws. While building the ark, and while as a priest he urged the people to repent their sins and return to God, he continued collaterally, as an economist, to advocate a restoration of the reductional system. By arguments and facts which would fill volumes, he demonstrated the superiority of the average labor-time standard of value; but in vain. The people would not relinquish Mammon and his retinue of hideous evils and sins. They adhered to the cloudy basis of *contingent* COST for determining the assize and purchasing power of a unit of the national paper money. They clung to it because it left prices to vary according to abundance and scarcity, or according to degrees of desire; and because it did not interfere with the greed of gain, the chances of acquiring exceptional riches by speculation, adven ture, credit, artifice, appropriation of the labor of others, etc.; but, on the contrary, legalized the thousand ways by which men might prey upon each other, and gratify their covetousness and lust.

Such strangers to God had they become, that, when he declared and confessed that reductionism was impossible without God—without faith and love to the true God—that even temporal and material prosperity *equitably distributed* could not be established without acknowledging God and God's exclusive title to natural values; but, that all things were possible with God, and through the motives His religion implanted, they laughed him to scorn and spurned his propositions.

They knew no motive but selfish desire and ambition, had taste but for the indulgence of dissoluteness and vice, no passion but such as gave rise to conflict and crime, and hence, when Noah told them his system would be slow in bearing fruit, and that those who enlisted in it must repress their evil inclinations, be actuated only by the spirit of love and sacrifice, and await the final benefit with patience, they were convinced he was an insane dreamer, fit only to be the object of children's play and teasing.

So the world continued in its sin and folly, which grew worse every day. It was whelmed and tossed by great wars and revolutions. For a long time the aristocracy of wealth held sway; but, attacked on every side by the envious and impatient poor whom economic customs and laws oppressed, they had to resort to the military force, and to rely on the support of the generals of the army. These were not slow to take advantage of this for their own aggrandizement, and they seized the government: made themselves kings and emperors, relying, in their turn, on their popularity among the common soldiery. At last the soldiers, having the most destructive weapons of war in their hands, after repressing every other rebellion, themselves rebelled; and sold the sovereignty of the world at auction every year.

Pestilence and famine were the proper consequences of such wide-spread violence and bloodshed; but these had no effect in turning men to God and virtue. On the contrary, they became more dissolute and cruel. The peoples lived in the midst of—and all took part in—robbery, fraud, forgery, embezzlement, prostitution, calumny, impiety, oppression, extortion, adulteration, monopoly, revenge, murder, and every other imaginable excess and crime.

Hence God said: "I will destroy man, whom I have created, from the face of the earth, and even beasts, ... creeping things, and .... fowls of the air; for it repenteth me I have made them. But Noah found grace before the Lord."

Therefore he alone and those with him were saved in the day of Almighty justice and indignation.

POSTSCRIPT.

NEW EDEN, OR HOW TO BE HAPPY ON EARTH.

I HAVE shown that rest of body and peace of mind constitute happiness. It now remains that I should also show *how* this rest and peace—and, therefore, this happiness—may be attained.

To do this I rely on two main facts: (1) that man is born a *natural* creature, but becomes a *spiritual* creature by receiving the Holy Spirit—the spirit of truth from God; (2) that the grace of the Holy Spirit modifies his soul, and even his natural body and mind, so as to make him, not indeed a different person, but so as to purify and exalt his intellect and his sentiments unto Christ and charity.

Thus there are two kinds of men: the natural and the spiritual. The first are those who remained in the fallen state of Adam; and the second are those who through Jesus Christ are raised again to a state of grace.

The natural man is an organism having (1) life, (2) sensation, (3) emotion, (4) thought or reason, and (5) an immortal soul.

The spiritual man is the same organism, whose inherent faculties and soul are made new, and illuminated by a superadded and divine element or influence.

I need not stop to marshal elaborate evidence of this division; for, the reader follows either the theories of material science, or the teachings of the church of Christ, and both of these guides agree on the matter of fact that there is one class of men who are (1) without God; that is to say, deny or repel God; (2) despair of immortality; and are (3) carnally minded; while there is another class who have (1) faith, (2) hope, and (3) charity.

The infidel scientists say the one class trust only to the light of their inherent senses and reason, and are actuated by animal instincts and selfish motives, all of which they regard as being according to nature or *natural;* and they say that the other class trust to the light of alleged revelation, that is to say, to an authority superior to their reason, and are actuated by a desire to merit heaven, and by a resolve to endure all suffering, and to sacrifice themselves in order to serve their brethren, and even their enemies, that they may please God—the which they regard as being contrary to nature—*unnatural.*

This is precisely what the theologians, and with them the religious scientists, affirm; and they add, it is not merely unnatural—it is supernatural—not possible without God, without his Holy Spirit, without Christ; and they add, further, that these "peculiar people" are those who believe in Christ-God, members of His church and none other.

I could cite hundreds of Scripture texts in which this distinction between the natural and spiritual man, the old man and the new man, the fallen and the raised again, the flesh and the spirit, the earthly and the divine man, the slaves of the devil and the free sons of God, is made in many ways; but this is unnecessary; for every good Christian knows them familiarly

I therefore may rightfully pass on to this twofold proposition: that the natural man cannot be happy here or hereafter; whereas the spiritual, that is to say, the truly religious man, is and will be ever happy.

This is, in other words, to say, that rest and peace, and therefore happiness, can be attained only in and through Christianity.

But while we study the happy, let us not lose sight of the unhappy.

The natural man is ever raging in discontent and unrest even in the midst of bodily health and worldly prosperity; while the spiritual man is ever

17

consoled even in the midst of material pain and destitution whatever may be the intensity of these.

Why is this? Simply because the one that disbelieves God, disobeys God, and rejects immortality and heaven, must be and is SELFISH; while the other believing, and hoping in God and the word of God, enlightened and moved by the Holy Spirit, must be and is CHARITABLE.

Thus, then, selfishness or egoism inevitably brings unhappiness, and charity assuredly procures happiness.

Selfishness is the main, the general characteristic of the natural man. True, the natural man is gregarious and sympathetic, but only in the feeble manner of the beasts, birds, and insects, to which he is always comparing himself, and in which (such as beavers and dogs, pigeons and eagles, bees and spiders) he willingly sees himself morally and intellectually—yes intellectually, asks Darwin—and by which he justifies his sensuality and covetousness.

The principal and worst element of selfishness is covetousness. The Scriptures are full of texts warning us of the many tribulations, the unrest, and the dangers of riches, and the desire of riches. Indeed the greed of riches is at the root of all evil; for it is the means eagerly sought by the sensual, the proud, the vain, in order to be able to satisfy their evil passions—their selfishness. How shall these ever have rest and peace? The man who, by the cunning artifices of speculation and traffic, or by the extortion of usury or monopoly, accumulates material wealth, and through this secures the privilege of idleness and bodily ease, will be disappointed, for he does not at the same time gain those spiritual riches wherein abideth peace for the soul. Covetousness, the first born of selfishness, implies extortion and usury, overreaching in trade, lies and fraud, hard-bargaining, appropriating the profit arising from the labor of others, which doings afford no rest or peace, but, on the contrary, solicitude, trouble, anxiety, envy of rivals, contention, vexation of heart, strain of mind, sleeplessness, fear, disappointment, many sorrows, and all the other cares and sins of the world. Selfishness and her eldest daughter, Covetousness, incite nations to wars of invasion and conquest, incite armies to commit pillage and levy contributions, incite princes and chieftains to usurpation. There is no rest and peace and therefore no happiness in the world because of covetousness. But even worse than causing war and its horrors, covetousness refuses labor its rightful reward—withholds just wages, and by this cruel injustice keeps generation after generation of millions of men in perpetual poverty, deprivation of rest and comfort, and, indeed, in extreme misery. Oh! who can count the number of victims which have thus been consigned to inflicted sickness and premature death, while covetousness stands by callously unconscious of having been guilty of innumerable murders. The covetous Judas betrayed the Lord for thirty pieces of silver; but he, less callous than the world, was driven by his tortured soul to suicide. Yet, even those who are insensible to the sufferings of others will feel their own; and so it is with the pursuers of riches who torture and destroy one another by their perpetual and merciless scrambles, manœuvres, snares, impostures, and spoliations.

Not only does selfishness incline us to commit those deeds of rapine, fraud, and oppression which covetousness of wealth suggests, but it has a proneness for indulgence in those vices, and the perpetration of those crimes which the other instincts and feelings of the natural man, when unsubdued, induce. All propensity and passion naturally seek actual satisfaction; and, if unrestrained by a higher motive, become habitual, morbid, and excessive. Thus the capabilities of nutrition, generation, sensation, and emotion God has given us, in order that we may preserve ourselves, and reproduce our kind, are abused and transformed into gluttony, lust, ostentation, vanity, pride, and envy, which, when opposed, give rise to anger, hate, revenge, boasting, calumny, insolence, violence, drunkenness, and libertinism.

Satan is selfish, and, therefore, the instigator of every moral evil; the prince of liars, thieves, and murderers.

Need I add, that, so long as selfishness is the leading motive of mankind in general, it will and must exclude that rest and peace, in which happiness consists, from the world?

Shall we not, therefore, seek happiness in the contrary of selfishness; that is to say, in charity?

Charity is the main, the general, characteristic of the spiritual man; for it is essentially religious, implies love and aspiration *to* God, and that grace from God, which, by its illumination and power, imparts all truth, and prompts man to seek himself in the angelic spheres; not down in the low range of his animal nature, but far above it.

Charity is not the mere benevolence, or generosity, or feeling of commiseration of him who succors or relieves others when he can conveniently do so, or who helps another from motives of friendship or policy; but charity is that heaven-imparted impulse, which feels its own origin, extends its radiance to all men, and reacting through works of piety, brotherhood, and sacrifice returns to God from whom it comes.

Vainly would I attempt to write an adequate description of the beauty and goodness of charity. To do so requires the eloquence of the inspired evangelists and apostles of Jesus Christ. It is in the Word of God, the example of Jesus and His saints, and the lessons of His church that we must study in order to understand the fulness of charity, and even then we should not know it if we did not also *feel* it, for it surpasseth all knowledge or learning. (Eph. iii. 19.)

This much, however, I must mention, that charity displays itself in affection, in brotherhood, in union, in tenderness, in meekness and modesty, in humility, in patience, in bearing and forbearing, in self-sacrifice, in gladly accepting the will of God when He dispenses temporal suffering, and in fulfilling His commandments, whatever trials and temptations are interposed to prevent us.

Among the traits of charity, growing out of its very essence, is a just regard for the rights of the poor, considered as being with us the children of the same Father who is in heaven, and as being with us equal heirs to all the natural bounties He has deposited in the natural world.

The solicitude of our Lord for the poor, and the rights of the poor, is manifested on every page of the New Testament. Before His advent it was a grievous sin to detain the laborer's wages, or to oppress the poor by a refusal of adequate wages; but the Lord, when he came, claimed for the toilers all the consequences of charity, one of which consequences is, that they must be loved and treated as associates, friends, and equals among men.

Charity by its proper nature is the original source of true liberty, equality, and fraternity, which are impossible among those who are actuated by ambition and avarice, or who admit the privilege of a few or even of the many to become tyrants and persecutors of others, or who glory in the acquisition and accumulation of unjust gain.

Charity, by the force of its inherent qualities, is necessarily a peace-maker; and by this same force brings men into union and harmony, community of labor and property, co-partnership of joy and suffering, faith and hope, for the charitable do not seek their own but other men's happiness.

Charity makes its votaries laborious; diligent workers with their own hands, doing that which is good, in order not to become a burden to society, and in order to relieve the wants of the brethren and others who cannot work.

Charity is not solicitous of making store of provision and raiment, nor treasure of gold and silver; but "seeks first the kingdom of God and His justice," that is: loves God and man, labors and distributes, obeys Christ and sacrifices self to Christ, fulfils commandments, precepts, and counsels of perfection, and relies on the promise that through this peace and rest, abundance and happiness "will be added unto him."

Charity is perfectly and fully described by our Lord when He says: "A new commandment I give unto you: that ye love one another as *I* have loved you." Think of the *model of love* which is thus proposed to your imitation, and then you will have some idea of the intensity and immensity of real Christian charity.

What a bold and glaring contrast there is between the natural man and the spiritual man: the egoism of the one, and the charity of the other; the endless fatigue and perpetual rage of the selfish, the rest and peace of the charitable.

Let us sum up the contrast in the words of St Paul.

"To be carnally minded is death, but to be spiritually minded is life and peace." (Rom. viii. 6.)

"The fruit of the spirit is love, joy, peace, patient suffering, gentleness, faith, meekness, temperance, chastity (Gal. v. 22); goodness, righteousness, justice, and truth." (Eph. v. 9, 10.)

"The works of the flesh are manifest, which are these: adultery, fornication, uncleanness, lasciviousness, luxury, idolatry, witchcraft, hatred, enmity, strife, sedition, heresies, envyings, murders, drunkenness, revellings and such like." (Gal. v. 19.)

I think it is now evident that charity is the principle on which political economy should be based.

The obstacle to this is irreligion.

I have already said that charity is religious; and now I add as a further proposition that charity is impossible without God and Faith, that the works and fruits of charity are impossible apart from the Christian religion.

The would-be philanthropists, who deny Christ and charity, imagine they can establish communities or reform the world by means of conventional agreements deduced from the operation of self-interests, or enacted by legislative power; but all their socialistic and communistic institutions must fall into corruption and expire, for they have within themselves the virus of selfishness. They may dream they have found charity in natural gregariousness and sympathy, or they may think to adopt the law of charity—the law of love, without receiving Christ; but in this they commit a fatal error.

It needs no argument to show that conduct proceeds from an adequate motive, and that the motive itself must exist. If we rely only on the natural constitution of man for motives sufficient to establish peace and rest, we are self-deluded; for the reason that that constitution, instead of having charity, is suffused with selfishness. The natural man does not feel or know charity. How then will selfishness be supplanted? How substitute charity or any other sufficient motive? Certainly arguments founded on self-interest will not do, for selfishness will not be divided against itself, will not destroy itself; and, however much convinced of its own efficacy, will continue to be what it is in itself, the principle of repulsion and division, avarice and enmity, corruption and sin.

A motive is required to induce men to banish selfishness, and give room in their hearts to love. What motive must this be? There is none other but FAITH. There is no adequate progenitor of genuine charity but religion.

Our mind must be certain, without shadow of doubt, that Jesus Christ is God, before we can absolutely rely on the truth and wisdom of His teaching, and before He can acquire over us that perfect influence and authority, which is necessary to sway us into obedience of His precepts and counsels of love.

We may, regarding Him only as a man, admire and approve His moral system, pronounce it beautiful, and be inclined to carry it into effect; but will never have the courage and perseverance necessary thereto; for the twofold reason that egoism would still have a stronghold in our hearts, and our conviction would still be less than certainty—would be a mere opinion, more or less strong, but ever subject to revision and reversal. We would fear to risk our welfare and happiness in a trial, apparently full of hardship, on the word of a man who, after all, was fallible, and who asks us to begin by making the great sacrifice of ourselves to the happiness of others.

But if this admiration of the beauty of Christ, this approval of His perfect doctrine, and the narration of His incomparable life, were to bring us to the recognition of His divinity—bring us to say this indeed is God—then we would not only be ready to obey Him with cheerfulness and confidence, but we would be eager to gain and return His love, receive the grace, and act with the power of the Holy Ghost, and thus be converted into the new man of charity.

When the rich young man, after claiming to have fulfilled the Mosaic law, asked Jesus what was lacking, then Jesus, beholding him, loved him, and said to him: "One thing thou lackest; go thy way, sell whatsoever thou hast and give to the poor, and thou shalt have treasure in heaven, and come, take up the cross and follow me." On this the young man went away grieved, for he had great possessions; and the disciples were astonished and murmured, saying among themselves, "Who then can be saved? And Jesus looking upon them said, things which are impossible with men are possible with God." *Therefore* the fulness of charity, of rest and peace, of happiness, are only possible with God, through Christ, by the Holy Ghost, and in the plenitude of the Christian religion.

Hear then the invitation of Christ Jesus: "Come unto me, all you who labor and are heavily laden, and I will refresh you. Take up my yoke upon you, and learn of me, because I am meek and humble of heart, and you will find *rest* to your souls, for my yoke is sweet and my burden light." (Matt. xi. 28, 29, 30.)

My argument will, no doubt, sound to the Christian reader as concluding that there must and should be a reign of Christ on earth, and that the proper destiny of man, so far as concerned with this mortal world, is the millennium described in Scripture.

This is certainly a true interpretation of my words.

Few Christians have analyzed the idea of the millennium. They generally content themselves with a very vague notion of it. A universal jubilee lasting for centuries, a time of happiness to all mankind, a world of goodness ruled by the Saviour. All agree that, in some way or other, there will be no misery, no tears, no war, no oppression, no wrong, and that love will reign supreme. There is no mistaking the Scriptures in these respects. If, however, you ask the questions: What that joy, that happiness will consist of? or, How the necessary abundance of good things for all will be produced, and on what principle distributed? or, By what plan and appliances a profusion of wealth will be created, and yet all injustice be prevented? you will find few ready to answer with any degree of precision. Few think of forming any exact conception of the social order that will then exist, or of what will then be the occupation of men. For instance, I have never met with any one who had deliberately considered the question whether, during the millennium, people will have to WORK. Yet, on this point, the Scriptures are clear. In the description of the day of the Lord, given by Isaiah and the other prophets, it is expressly stated not only that men will eat and dress, and live in houses, but also that they will *do the work* necessary now for obtaining food, clothes, and habitations. They will have and use the necessary tools and implements. They will beat their swords into *plowshares and pruning* hooks. They will *build.* They will *plant and reap.* (Is. ii.) "Mine elect shall long enjoy the WORK of their hands," saith the prophet in the very passage in which he describes the New Jerusalem. (Is. lxiv. 21.) An hundred other texts might be quoted; but this is enough. Hence, we must bring into our image of the millennium—*men at work;* tilling the soil, building houses, weaving stuffs, fashioning tools, etc.

But the millennium will be a state of unmixed happiness, of unrestricted joy to all, though work will be done. We will have to combine the picture of mankind at work with that of mankind enjoying perfect happiness. These two conditions must be made to fit each other.

Here is a puzzle for the philosophers and political economists, who ignore God and the word of God. How can their laws of trade, of hiring, of rents, of interest, of profits, of capital, of supply and demand, of fluctuating prices, of buying cheap and selling dear, of the relations of master and servant, of buying labor at starving prices, etc., be adapted to a system where, though work is necessary, it shall not be painful, make no one miserable, deprive no one of adequate rest and leisure, be no source of wrong, fraud, or oppression, but rather of pleasure? It is evident that all the means, customs, and laws whereby the few are enabled to take advantage of the many, whereby one builds and another inhabits, must in the millennial day be abolished. Certainly that day will not arise so long as the present laws promoting individual appropriation and accumulation are allowed to stand; for, while they last, the inequalities and wrongs which now torture the millions must continue.

What then? Simply this, that in those days every man—yes, every man and woman without exception —will not only have to work, but to work as a real *bona fide* producer—a producer of that which is good for the commonwealth—a producer bringing his products to the common store for general distribution and exchange, on the principle that labor is the measure of value; that the labor IN a product (not the product) is what gives title to a reward, and, therefore, is the true basis for estimating that reward.

On this basis will be found a sure and practical foothold for *equality*. On this equality there will be no place for drones, but only for industry; and since equal industry implies universal industry, so universal industry, or all men being real producers, implies abundance for all; and abundance with equality implies a full measure of recreation, rest, and peace for every laborer.

The combined laws of love and labor admit of no other realization.

Work—but be not selfish or avaricious—distribute in love.

Work—but do not snatch to thyself the work of others—the laborer is worthy of his reward.

Work—but do not in vanity and egoism value your labor higher than that of others.

Work—but take only what is due to thy work itself, and exact not what God has given and is due to Him alone.

Work—but love, and do not attempt to lay up treasure in order to live the life of an unproductive idler, or of the extortive miser.

Work—but seek not riches and its luxuries. Ye cannot serve God and mammon. "Seek ye first the kingdom of God and His righteousness, and all these things" (*i.e.*, abundance, rest, and peace) "will be added unto you."

What, after all, will be the millennium but the simple fact of the conversion of men, without excepting one, to *practical* Christianity? What, but the advent of a state of the world, during which every man will live so as to be worthy of taking immediate possession of his eternal inheritance through Christ? The unanimity of mankind in Christianity is what of itself will make the millennium—constitute the new Eden of Labor.

But, alas! "Oh Lord, how long?" When will thy

holy charity be unanimously practised by every man
of all kindreds and tongues?

Thy Scriptures reply. "The day and hour when
thou wilt come knoweth no man, no, not the angels
of heaven, but the Father only."

While thy people wait, shall they be indolent?
Nay—for this much they do know: thou wilt not
come till they have prepared the way. Till, by
thy grace, they have succeeded in this immense
work, the world, and they with it, must suffer—have
no rest or peace—incur all the consequences of sin
—*groan* with the orgies of the great and the miseries
of the lowly. Therefore, they will strive, endure
and pray without relaxation, having the certainty
that the greater their patience and fidelity in the
fulfilment of this duty of preparing thy way, the
greater will be their reward. It is the heavenly
design that the world have happiness, though it is
free to reject it; but if the world refuse to be happy,
by the only course through which happiness is
possible here and hereafter, it is promised that the
faithful and true who suffer here shall attain beatitude hereafter. The world cannot deprive them of
this final and heavenly happiness, by any conceivable
act or artifice. Those who labor to prepare the way
for the coming of the Lord, though they expire
before the work is done for the world, will not be
kept waiting in the grave. They will instantly
enjoy the Vision of God. Eye has not seen nor ear
heard, neither can the imagination of man conceive
what are the joys the beatific vision will impart.
Hence there are no words in human language to
describe it adequately. This much, however, can be
affirmed of Heaven: that there we shall feel no more
passions, but only perpetual and progressive delights
—that no heavenly delight will ever satiate—that
Heaven's delights will accrue in succession and by
addition; and each of them will come to the blest
by an ineffable surprise. While they enjoy the
present vision and ecstasy they will not be able by

any effort even of their transcendent and celestially illumined minds to foresee or infer what the next insight and ecstasy will be. Each will impress them as not to be exceeded—as supreme and ultimate. Hence no desire will precede any of the stages of beatitude. They will constitute a series of immeasurable raptures ever extending broader, deeper, higher, and with increasing glory, without any one of them diminishing or impairing those that have previously accrued; but all subsisting in their own peculiar vividness. Respectively they will be as different, while as simultaneous, as the enjoyment of the distinct senses and faculties of the human self, though infinitely purer and perfectly delectable. Their number will be illimitable, while all will consist in knowing and enjoying God as He is, in some glory of His inexhaustible perfection.

18

APPENDIX.

EXPLANATION OF THE MONOGRAM.

MASTERS of political economy are not unanimous when answering the question : What is the proper definition of that science ? *Quesnay*, the great father of political economy, he who first conceived the possibility of a body of doctrine on the matter, regarded it as "the science of the natural rights of men in their social relations so far as these concerned wealth or property." *Adam Smith* no doubt conceived it to be " the science of the nature and causes of the wealth of nations." *Condillac* held that it is "the science of commerce." *J. B. Say* expressly defines it as "the science which treats of the production, distribution, and consumption of wealth." *MacLeod*, the last author, well versed in the doctrines best accredited among the professional teachers of the science, says: " Economics is the science which treats of the laws which govern the relations of *exchangeable* values." According to his idea, exchange is the central point around which the whole science revolves, and to the understanding of which its study gravitates. To this object production, consumption, agriculture, manufactures, and carrying are merely subordinate or accessory.

If I had the power to decide, I would say that " economics is the science of the principles or laws God has ordained, in nature and revelation, for the distribution or apportionment of the results of labor, that is to say, of wealth." I have shown why and how I regard the exchangeable value of wealth as justly determinable only by the measure of average

labor time.   In one word I would therefore say:
" Political economy is the science of the fundamental
rights of labor."

But this has been discussed in the preceding pages;
and my present purpose is only to present a monogram of economics as *now* practically operative under
the laws which now govern the evolution, reservoirs
and channels of wealth.

It seems to me that this monogram presents to the
eye a good and true view of the principal features
and movements which the political economy of the
schools teaches and accredits.

I would first direct attention to the *reservoir*
furthest to the left in connection with the one furthest to the right.   They are connected by *tubes*, one
of which is the suction-pipe of a pump, the handle of
which is held and worked by a man: a personifica-
tion of LABOR.   This suction-pipe is marked REPRO-
DUCTION.   The reservoir on the left is CAPITAL, and
is primarily supplied from nature, which, without
cost, pours into it her wealth.   This natural wealth,
through the efforts of labor, is drawn out (extracted),
pumped up (converted) into a reservoir of commo
dities (or wages) necessary for the SUBSISTENCE or
reproduction of the laborer himself.   A surplus, not
needed for the immediate subsistence or reproduction
of the laborer himself, overflows; and is carried, by
the conduit marked *Economy No.* 1, back to the reservoir of capital.   This surplus flows back to capital in the shape of *made things*, such as materials laid
by, provisions stored, cottages built, articles manufactured, money saved, in so much as the laborer is
allowed to have the results of his own toil, and sets
them apart for future use.   Thus the reservoir of
capital becomes the recipient of two kinds of things,
viz.: (1) raw or natural and (2) manufactured or artificial objects, the latter being always a combination
of the work of man with the work of God.

In the beginning there were no other draw-offs,
tubes, reservoirs or consumers between the reservoir

of capital and that into which the laborer cast the results of his toil. All the surplus he made, and allowed to flow back into capital, continued to be his own property. All capital was owned by the laborer who produced it.

But from this fact of ownership which was, by a violation of God's will, allowed to include the natural value of capital, and from the common consent that it was just and proper to secure and defend (1) the usurpation of an ownership in natural values, and (2) the right of individuals to dispose as they pleased of what was conceded to be their property, other reservoirs and draw-offs were logically and artfully formed. These were the reservoirs and draw-offs of TAXES, USURY, RENT, and PROFIT. Look at the monogram, and you will see they get all their supply from the efforts of labor, which at first had appropriated the ownership of natural values, but only so far as combined with labor values. Observe that the draw-offs of taxes, usury, rent, and profit, marked A, B, C, and D, are inserted between the lifting lever and valve F, worked by the laborer, and the draw-off E, through which he received the reward of his toil. Thus the fruits of that toil must firstly supply and fill the tubes or draw-offs A, B, C, and D, before supplying the tube E, or wages-fund—that is to say, supply the exigencies of taxes, usury, rent, and profit, before reluctantly yielding to the necessity of supplying subsistence to that strength and skill on which all depends to make natural wealth available and fit to be used by human creatures.

Between the reservoirs of taxes, usury, rent, profit, and capital there are conduits marked Economy 2, 3, 4, and 5, which are so disposed as to carry off the surplus left unconsumed by the four first named reservoirs to the fifth one, which is capital. Hence when we examine the arrangement of these reservoirs and conduits, the height at which the conduits marked Economy are placed, their necessary effect, and the

18*

order of antecedence and subsequence in which they stand, we at once perceive that:—

Usury is drawn from the leavings of taxes.

Rent is drawn from the portion of production usury and taxes have, either voluntarily or involuntarily, failed to consume.

Profit is drawn in the same way from the portion of produce left unconsumed by taxes, usury, and rent.

Wages are the leavings of taxes, usury, rent, and profit. (See draw-off E and conduit No. 1.)

Capital is the *economy* or surplus saved from immediate consumption according to the relative precedence, power, craft, prudence, and opportunities of government, usury, rent, profit, and lastly of labor.

The reservoir of capital is imagined as containing *all* that can be denoted by that name, *no matter who may be the owner*—all that is saved from being consumed by the current support of the State, the usurers, and from the devouring requisitions of comfort and luxury. It is apparent that very little of the contents of the reservoir of capital can possibly belong to labor, though before God, labor is entitled to it all.

Each of these reservoirs *varies in capacity* according to the fluctuations of industry and commerce. So also do the delivering tubes *change in size* according to these fluctuations. It is remarkable that the tubes and reservoirs of usury and rent are being continually enlarged. As to profit, its tube and reservoir expand and contract with wonderful elasticity. By their automatic elasticity, all the reservoirs are kept up to the *level of circulation*. When any one of them, in consequence of the increase or diminution of loss or gain, supplies more or less to those who enjoy its share, they feed and feast, or, suffer and depart, become more or less numerous, according to the volume of that supply.

LABOR is the only creator of *exchangeable* value; the only *cost* of any commodity. This is generally admitted by the masters of political economy; but, most times, they cloud the admission by ignoring comparative *time* as a necessary factor in estimating the value of labor, and by enlarging the meaning of the word so as to include even the conception of a plan, a manœuvre in exchanges, or a mercantile adventure, and the like.

It is apparent that the draw-offs of taxes, usury, rent, and profit must all be filled to the full extent of their delivering capacity before a drop of subsistence can be raised to the height of the last draw-off (E) which delivers the wages-fund to the laborers. If the consumers of taxes, usury, rent, and profit could, they would so enlarge the draw-offs that nothing would flow over to labor; but, since it is by its efforts that their own reservoirs are supplied, they are forced to restrict their draw-offs so as to afford at least a *minimum* of subsistence to the laborers. They are ever striving to bring down the wages-fund to this minimum. They greet the invention of labor-saving machines, not because these tend to increase the amount and cheapness of subsistence, and of other things good for the poor, but because they may procure comforts, luxuries, and excesses, at less cost, and by feeding a lesser number of laborers. I admit there are superficial circumstances, such as decrease of demand or dearness of raw material, which, at a given moment, compel a reduction of wages; but the purpose of usury, rent, and profit to enlarge themselves at the expense of labor, though individual consciences may feel no reproach, is the general and bottom cause of the superficial and immediate circumstances.

It is but natural that, pushed to the extreme, this tendency gives rise to unions and co-operations of laborers against profit, and *strikes* against the withholding of living wages.

This tendency, in its double evolution of reduction of wages, which the increase of population assists, and the reduction of the number of workmen, which

the invention of labor-saving machines permits, in-
duces also PAUPERISM and EMIGRATION.

Thus arise the most disagreeable of all the questions that can be propounded to political economists.
What is the law, and what are the effects of the increase of POPULATION? What proportion of labor
should be appropriated to *necessary, commodious*, and
luxurious production respectively? What to the fine
arts? How much and in what specialities (if any) to
pernicious works, doings and products? What ratio
of capital should be devoted to wages? How much
production may be safely consumed unreproductively,
or how much does reproductive investment absolutely require? What of the *eight-hour* movement?
granges? woman's work? children's work? etc.

Since the slow infusion of christianity, the principle of charity has been influencing, more and more
deeply, the peoples of Europe. Hence, labor has
advanced from slavery to serfdom, from serfdom to
wagedom, and is now moving, through wagedom, to
the freer life of piece-work—whence it will doubtless wholly emancipate itself from masters—then
rise to *co-operative* JOB-*work*, and finally attain the
height of average labor-time, made the common
standard of all value.

TAXES are the contributions of labor for social
and national purposes.

Would that they were now righteously levied and
used only according to that purpose.

Whether first in historical order or not, the reservoir of taxes has logical precedence of the subduc-
tions from labor made by usury, rent, and profit.
Taxes support government. Society is hardly conceivable without government. The inference is, that
taxes cannot be dispensed with. But *how much* shall
they be? what for? how and to whom should taxes
be distributed? what taxes are just and proper?
how and on what basis should they be levied? what
is their effect on the exchangeable value of land or
goods? are questions which political economy can-

not avoid, since they relate to the rights of labor, the wealth or capital produced by labor, and national prosperity.

The most favorable view that can be reasonably taken of taxes is, that, with the exception of a few of them which produce public wealth and morality, the rest are either necessary evils or positive wrongs. The *productive* are those levied for making roads, bridges, and canals, deepening rivers and ports, lighting cities, and other such works. The *necessary* are those for adequately supporting a police, a judiciary, armies and navies, a fire department, and the like. The positively *injurious* are those which discriminate between the objects of taxation, such as protective tariffs and licenses; those which press heavily upon certain kinds of property, while some favored private property or business is exempted, or those which, though bearing on all kinds, are unequally imposed; and those which, though to a certain extent necessary, are levied in *excess* to furnish bounties, sinecures, and *booty* to corrupt and useless officers and other favorites of the State.

The consumer of taxes is the sovereign; he who makes the laws and holds the sword of power. Some would like me to say the sword of justice, but alas! this term would not always agree with the fact. Whether the sovereign is hereditary or elective, a monarch or a representative body composed of many members and departments, is immaterial; for, in either case the sovereign entity is properly personified as sitting on a throne and holding the book and the sword. The book defines, and the sword enforces the economic system of the country; they guarantee and defend the acquisition, enjoyment, and transmission of property. The book determines the nature and validity of contracts, and the sword compels the parties to a strict observance of their legal promises.

The book, on its first or constitutional page, professes to secure to all life, liberty, and the pursuit of happiness—it almost says the rights of labor. When, however, we study it, we soon learn that usury, rent, and profit, no matter how extortionate and exorbitant, no matter whether they are derived from a righteous title, or from the usurpation of natural things, or from some other primary wrong, are regarded by it as just rewards of labor. Then it graciously declares that wages must also be so regarded. Instead of translating the Scripture to say, "the laborer is worthy of his *reward*"—which might be interpreted to mean *all* he has justly earned, all that his work has added to the material used, the version is made to say "the laborer is worthy of his *hire*," which conveys a very different idea. The book of legislation, therefore, recognizes wages only as the rate of remuneration *freely* consented to between a laborer and an employer or master. "Freely" means that if labor will not take the leavings of taxes, usury, rent, and profit, it is free to starve, there being no alternative. This is what the economists call free trade and human rights—a guaranty that every man shall have his own—shall possess and dispose of his person, property, and labor according to his own will uncontrolled by the caprice and uncoerced by the power of any other man. They mean, however, and even say, that this liberty and guaranty exist only in so far as the book defines and permits.

The book promises the dispensation of justice; but when we come to ascertain what this means, we find it is the enforcement of the privileges and advantages of usury, rent, and profit over labor. It is the justice of Shylock in disregard of the Sinaic decalogue, the Christian precepts and the Christian counsels of perfection.

It institutes or sanctions the appropriation and transmission in perpetuity of natural wealth, such as wild lands, mines, water-falls, mineral springs, fisheries, etc.

It ratifies rapine, such as prize of war, or the capture from enemies of chattels, lands, and prisoners;

and endows individuals with the right of holding them as property.

It confirms the gain or advantage any *hirer* derives from the work of an organism of combined or concerted labor, on condition of only paying each laborer as if he worked by himself, and as if nothing were due to the multiplying force and effect of united action. I mean the united action which the economists, by a singular contradiction, denote by the phrase "Division of Labor."

I have written the word monopoly under the throned and diademed consumer of taxes; for from his book proceed, and on his sword rely, all monopolies and privileges, the name of which is legion: such as charters with exclusive license; enterprises favored with premiums, bounties, and subsidies; tariffs and duties protective or discriminating; national banks authorized to issue currency guaranteed by the State; unequal taxation levied so as to favor or exempt particular interests; contracts for supplying the State with material or service, or for constructing public works awarded to favorites on conditions and rates which defraud and spoliate the public treasury.

From these taxes, raised by virtue of this book and sword, officials and their satellites are enriched, armies and navies are maintained, national wars are waged, custom-houses and forts are built to girt the land. True, in the midst of all, much of what is good and needful is accomplished; but it is drowned in an ocean of abuse and fraud.

Hence political economy is called upon to consider the facts which bear upon these points, so far as they effect the production, exchange, and appropriation of the wealth of nations.

USURY follows taxes in logical order, though we can well see how profit and rent were probably antecedent in order of time, and how the enriched merchant and landlord sold out to devote his realized capital exclusively to the perpetration of usury, and

himself to a life of ease, idleness, and unlimited indulgence. Usury is the final pursuit or vocation of
all those who have made net and great fortunes from
the favors of the State, the adventures of commerce,
and speculations in land. By becoming a usurer
one yields his place in the State, in commerce, in
land ownership, to new adventurers, commissioned
to demand money in the name of the State, that they
may embezzle it, or use it for their speculations in
commerce, manufactures, and agriculture. Usury is
the *razor* that denudes the head and face of labor of
every vestige of hair the *scissors* of taxes have left.
Usury exacts good security, makes herself safe, while
her borrowers are more liable to fail. The result is
the general enlargement of the wealth of the usurer.
Her tendency is to make every other pursuit tributary to her. She becomes continually more and more
plethoric. Her sphere is that of *national debts* and
bonds and CURRENCY, banks and banking, insurance,
dealing in bills of exchange and well secured notes,
the purchase of prosperous stocks, and all questions
of CREDIT and FINANCE. It is in this sphere that
political economy studies speculation in *stocks* and
money, not mistaking the imitators who speculate in
the money-market on a small capital, and who risk
all on a large venture for real usurers.

RENT, seated *key* in hand in the midst of luxury,
looks complacently upon Labor cultivating his farms,
or on Profit occupying his houses. Watching these
and collecting his rentals is the only business that
disturbs his equanimity and pleasures. His studies
in political economy (if he studies at all) comprise
the sections which treat of the TENURE of land—the
causes which influence the price of land and the rate
of RENTS—the rise and fall of cities—the kinds and
methods of AGRICULTURE best suited to his country's
soil, climate, and staples—the advantages and disadvantages of *meteyer* and *cottier* tenancy—and of large
and small farms. Anxious to increase his fortune by
purchasing lands or houses that will become more

valuable in the course of time from the industry of
others, he surveys the country and the development
of its resources in order to invest in localities towards
which a tide of population is flowing, and in which
improvements are progressing.

Political economy, as taught by the accredited masters, in accord with his feelings and supposed interest,
furnishes him with the principle by which the rate
of rent he may exact is to be determined—" Bare
subsistence for the cultivator, and all the surplus for
the proprietor."

This fact enables us to class under the caption of
rent not only agriculture but also MANUFACTURES.
Rent is disguised or enveloped in the income which
owners of farms derive from the work of hired agricultural laborers, and which owners of *factories*, and
the like, derive from the service of their wagemen.
Whether they lease their farms or factories to others,
or carry them on themselves, the nature and source
of the revenue is essentially the same; it is derived
from the working and occupancy or other use made
by others than themselves, of their landed or other
property and its accessories; and it is also the part
of the product left to the owner after deducting the
mere support of the cultivator or other operative.

When the farmer or manufacturer himself works,
he does so in a double capacity—his earnings, in that
case, include two elements: he receives a part as
laborer and a part as owner of the property used;
but his hired man only get the *minimum* allowed to
labor. Whatever more is produced by his work, it
is taken by the owner; and therefore this part is
really rent.

To the category of rent also belongs the income
derived from LAND AND WATER CARRYING by the
owners of wagons, ships, and the like. The same
remarks I have made in regard to rent, apply to
freight and fare.

PROFIT is all that one or both parties to an
exchange receive in excess of the *cost* of the things

19

exchanged and the average *wage* necessary for the support of the transferer, according to the proportion of time he consumes in rendering service to the transferee. In one word, all that a dealer is entitled to is *cost* and laborer's *wages*—what more he gets is *profit*.

In the monogram Profit is represented differently from Usury and Rent in this, that they are reclining or seated, but he is standing. He is necessarily busy and active—runs to and fro—follows COMMERCE—travels by ship and rail—buys and sells—frequents the marts and markets—is ever on the alert for a bargain—speculates on demand and supply, on fashion and credulity, on scarcity and abundance—spreads his nets and snares—stretches his credit, and stakes his solvency on the chances of uncertain transactions.

The distinguishing trait of profit is that it is made by two acts: (1) buying and (2) selling; or, what is the same thing, the double act of *barter* or *exchange*. All other income is from labor, taxes, usury, or rent; and I note, as I pass on, that besides these there are other modes of acquiring property, according to some special and discretionary provision of *law*, such as (1) preoccupancy, (2) prescription, (3) gift, (4) legacy, (5) inheritance, (6) wager-won, (7) treasure-trove, (8) capture, and (9) salvage. These nine are the *origin* of most of the abuses and wrongs of which labor complains.

Politically, the votaries of profit are divided between two parties: that of PROTECTION and that of FREE TRADE.

CAPITAL now presents itself again and may be better understood. It consists of all valuable things or qualities of things appropriated or otherwise possessed by man wherewith he may reproduce himself, derive subsistence, utility, comfort, or pleasure—lands, houses, cattle, machines, tools, implements, furniture, food, clothing, fuel, carriages, vessels, roads, books, MONEY, and many other objects, even strength, health, knowledge, education, skill, genius, virtue, nothing being excepted but what is so abundant, so available to all, so common that, though appropriated to any possible extent, it would command no *price*, as the air, the sea, etc Even the air or sea, if appropriated so as to exclude its use unless for a price, would thereby be converted into capital. Suppose the military navy of a nation were so overpowering that it could forbid the use of the sea to all vessels except those who paid for a license to do so ; the sea would then be a part of that nation's capital. Perhaps some way may be discovered of exacting payment to appropriators for the air we breathe. It would thereby become property or capital ; the two terms are almost synonymous.

Every specific piece of capital involves seven kinds of value ; (1) a *natural* value which is God's property, (2) a *labor* value which is man's property ; (3) an *extortional* value depending on the proportion in which it is subjected to monopoly, for in every thing there is a degree of monopoly ; (4) a *passional* value, which is according to taste or desire ; (5) a *competitive* value, which depends upon demand and supply and the extent to which it is allowed to be made an object of free trade ; (6) a *cost* value, which determines the profit or loss made upon it through purchase and sale or exchange ; and (7) an *exchangeable* value, which is the reduction of the six others into one, and comprises all their effects expressed by the term *price*, or market-price, or the adage "a thing is worth what it will bring."

Wealth or value is both POSITIVE *and* RELATIVE. Price is the exponent of the sum of elements, contained in each thing or service, so far only as it is relative.

Natural value consists in the intrinsic qualities which render things or actions of persons and things fit for human uses. Of these qualities two are particularly notable in political economy, for they are factors in every problem this science is called upon to solve. These are (1) durability and (2) consumability. Both exist in every particle of capital, but in proportions inversely related. *Durability* is the largest proportion of the value of land, of gold and the like; and enables the appropriators of such things to derive a perennial revenue from them, through rent or usury. It is, to them, the inexhaustible purse of Fortunatus, which, every time it was emptied, filled again of itself or from a talismanic virtue requiring no labor or other effort of its possessor. Though, by rent or usury, an appropriator of land or gold may have recovered all the labor-value ever put into it, ten times over, his right to own it as capital and to derive revenue from it remains intact. Now it would seem as if this could not happen when the quality of *consumability* greatly predominates in the thing or service appropriated, as it does in the value of food, clothing, fuel, and the like. Its appropriators cannot get pay for it more than once: but customs and laws have established and secured the draw off of profit; and enabled the appropriators to obtain, directly or indirectly, a bonus or premium even greater than that of rent or usury, out of the labor of the final consumer.

Labor-value, as I have abundantly shown in the first part of this book, consists of usefulness added or facilitated by labor for the benefit of the consumer of things or service. This value is created by three modes of effort: (1) Mono-manual effort; (2) Associational effort; (3) Social effort. (1) *Mono-manual* labor value is that which the work of a single person independently creates when it increases utility or facilitates consumption: *Ex.* a woodman may fell a tree and cut it up without help. (2) *Associational* labor-value is that which is imparted by the united or concerted labor of several persons: *Ex.* the united efforts of several are necessary to raise the framework of a house or bridge. (3) *Social value* is that imparted to property through public works and through improvements caused by local increase of population, or is the abundance created by production multiplied or labor saved through the progress of art, whereby labor may be liberated from one kind of work and applied to another: *Ex.* Land becomes more valuable by opening a road for the exportation of its products; the art of printing saves the labor of copying and multiplies books and makes them for a lesser price than they previously cost.

But nearly all the values—the prolific and economical benefits—created by *associated* and *social* labor, are intercepted by the draw-offs of taxes, usury, rent, and profit to be almost entirely consumed in procuring comfort, luxury, and plethora for those who possess the reservoirs into which these draw offs flow. *The* mass of positive wealth, capital, and value is enormously increased. Indirectly the laborer gets a small share of the benefits of general progress; *but though,* through the advance of science and art, *he can make* ALL *he consumed by working* THREE *hours per day,* TEN, TWELVE, *or* SIXTEEN *hours per day all the year round hardly suffice to procure it.*

We have already seen how capital may be made either *r*eproductive or *un*reproductive. It is the way of the CONSUMPTION of wealth which determines its character in this respect.

There is, however, a kind of capital which, in itself, is *un*reproductive, but which is never consumed, and is, therefore, a species by itself. It is MONEY. The disputes among the economists and financiers about the nature and basis of money involve so many questions that even a statement of the points in controversy would be too lengthy for this monogram. I will only give my own definition of the thing itself. Money is a valuable object, OR a *title* to some property or right, which (by common consent and reasons of common interest) is accepted by any and every person, for any and every object or service.

The tubes in the monogram represent the functions of money. Being a mere evidence of *title* to property, money is nothing in itself. It is the evidence of the obligation which every person in the world, or a nation has tacitly or expressly contracted to furnish the bearer a certain amount of property on demand. As such, it is an excellent medium of exchange, for since its transfer conveys title to any and everything, it dispenses him who passes or transfers it from delivering any particular property to him who receives it. The latter uses it in the same manner as the former did, and so on *ad infinitum*. It is like a warehouse receipt, but the warehouse from which it is issued comprises all the property of the world, or at least of a nation. It is also like water, it flows through the tubes of *circulation*, instead of the property which it transfers. It flows from reservoir to reservoir with commutative fluidity. Both it and they are *elastic* in the same proportion, so that when its volume is enlarged the tubes and reservoirs enlarge, and when it is reduced they contract. Since all the reservoirs are connected, the fluid circulation always stands at the same level in all of them, no matter how little or how much each reservoir may contain. From the fact that money is a *title deed* to any and all property which any and all owners may seek to exchange, it follows that, as the number of units of money is increased or diminished while the quantity of property remains the same, each unit becomes a title for *less* or *more* of the sum total of property held for exchange, according to the variation of the number of units in circulation. If it is the volume of exchangeable property that is increased or diminished while the number of units of money remains unchanged, the same relative effect is produced. These changes, if slow and gradual, are harmless, but if a change in the volume of currency is sudden, it may make so great a difference (between the amount of property that was required to discharge a debt at the time that it was incurred and the property required to discharge it when it falls due) as to ruin the creditor if the change be to less, or the debtor if it be to more. Again, though currency is wonderfully elastic, and each of its units or fractions

is a title to more or less property, according to their
number; yet, if the number is very small, it would
be necessary (if the currency is metallic) to divide
the units into parts so minute as to be practically
useless.   There was an approximation to this in the
century which preceded the discovery of the Mexi-
can and Peruvian mines.   No better remedy was then
thought of than official adulteration of the gold and
silver, and a large coinage of ponderous copper.   If,
on the contrary, the number of units (whether of
paper or metal) were inordinately increased, each
unit would be a title to so small a part of the mass
of property that the whole and its divisions would
be too cumbersome for the uses and functions of
currency.   An instance of this was the iron money
of Sparta.

It would help us to understand money, if we were
to figure it to ourselves as a CARRIER.   For instance,
we might allegorically personify it under the form
of a flock of *Hippogriffs* engaged in bearing property, goods and chattels, from one person to another :
each Hippogriff or unit gaining or losing strength or
carrying power in exact proportion to the increase
or decrease of the *work* required of the whole flock,
provided they are always sufficiently numerous to
attend to every service required, whether that service
be small or great.   A development of the *details* of
this allegorical view would correct several popular
errors on the nature and functions of money ; but the
space I have here at my disposal is too limited for
this, and I must therefore defer it to another occasion.

But besides being (1) a *title* to merchandise, (2) a
vehicle or *carrier* of merchandise, money is also (3)
in itself merchandise.   All other things continuing
to be demanded and supplied as before, if the supply
of money is increased while the number and amount
of transactions for which it is needed remain the same
or are diminished, its value or purchasing power and
the rate of interest will fall.   The contrary will
happen if the supply of money is diminished, while

the number of transactions remains the same or is increased ; also if the supply of money remains the same, but the number and amount of transactions are increased. Hence money is merchandise ; for it is bought, sold, and hired, its fluctuations are precisely those of merchandise, and governed by the same laws.

When our Lord wished to draw and show the line between secular and holy things, he pointed out money as the representative of all that is secular or temporal. This sphere he intrusted to Cæsar, and gave him (the State) dominion over it. Hence the State can make money and the concerns it represents to be blessings or curses according to the wisdom or foolishness of expediency and policy. All the rest he reserved as sacred to God : viz., conscience, religion, morals, education—everything that concerns the individual mind and soul. These are inviolable. The State has no right to interfere with them—no authority over them. On the contrary, the State itself must submit and conform itself therein. He taught that he and his church alone had jurisdiction in this supreme and holy sphere, the great law of which is to obey God rather than man : suffer death rather than lose our soul. But alas! for the sake of Cæsar's money and the material goods it represents and purchases, we refuse to render unto God that which is God's, and surrender even our immortal souls to the world and hell—wrest, by force and false pretences, the labor and portion of our brethren—and recognize no law but Cæsar's book and sword ; and would fain evade even these to indulge the perversity of corrupted nature.

Now viewing the monogram *generally*, I have only four or five more short remarks to make before I stop.

1. The same person may cumulate several sources of income or several kinds of capital. He may be an officer of government receiving a salary out of the taxes while being a usurious lender of funds, a

lessor of lands, houses, machines, ships, carriages, or chattels, and a speculator buying and selling at the risk of losing or gaining from the rise or fall of prices. This cumulation may and does vary in multitudes of individual cases which are more or less complicated. It would be tedious to state merely the most common instances. Even the poor laborer may earn his wages and, at the same time, draw a driblet of usury made on his deposits in the savings bank.

2. The size and proportion of *each* draw-off and reservoir may be and is continually changing—their contents vary from day to day—while one enlarges the other contracts, except the opposite reservoirs of capital and labor which maintain without much alteration their respective proportions to each other and to the whole, while, however, the tendency of capital is to a maximum share, and the force of the system is to reduce labor to a minimum allotment.

3. The total population, by force of natural law and the volume of capital, by force of social laws, would, *if not hindered*, increase concurrently by increments which would progress in *geometrical* ratio, but this tendency is opposed and its course impeded by causes which according to political economists are either REPRESSIVE or PREVENTIVE.

The repressive causes are the most numerous. I will only mention a few, already alluded to in preceding pages.

(i.) There is a prevailing spirit of cupidity and pride, selfishly seeking riches and power through public spoliation and war, or private artifices and violence, by which millions of lives are diverted from reproductive industry and finally sacrificed.

(ii.) Labor is compelled to devote itself principally to such works as provide for the gratification of the desires and tastes of the capitalists, so that only the number of workmen needed for this purpose are allowed to work and live.

(iii.) Though there is a constant increase of capital

appropriated to the support of labor, the difference between total population and total laborers and
between total capital and total labor-fund is constantly changing, so that the share of wealth accruing to capitalists is continually becoming not only
greater in amount but greater in proportion.

(iv.) There is constantly increasing difference between the number of wagemen actually *employed* and
the number actually U*N*employed—the increase being
on the side of the latter; and this, for those who are
employed, implies *less* wages; while for those who,
at one time or another, are unemployed it implies *no*
wages; hence, pauperism, disease, and inordinate
mortality.

(v.) Necessity drives men, women, and children,
into deleterious manufactures and other unhealthy
works, or to premature and excessive work.

(vi.) The control of the application of new discoveries and inventions, for saving labor and multiplying products, enables the appropriating class to
dispense with a still greater proportion of the laboring class, so that the very fact of progress in science
and art is perverted to increase the proportion of
unemployed hands.

(vii.) Since repressive causes operate to the inflic-
tion of death only because of an excess of population,
composed of unemployed and starving, or deleteri-
ously and excessively worked, wagemen, it is manifest that the number of the wage people is always
ahead of the amount of the wage-fund that capital
has devoted to their subsistence.

(viii.) The fear of aggravating poverty by attempting to raise a family, incites thousands to commit,
by indirect and even direct means, abortion and in-
fanticide.

These repressive causes are summed up in the
Scriptures in three words, War, Famine, Pestilence,
or in one . . . Murder.

I know only one cause opposed to the *natural* increase of population, which may, in contradistinction

to the preceding, he considered as PREVENTIVE. It is that voluntary and holy chastity which is counselled by religion and which once covered the face of Europe with convents and monasteries.

4. Now let me try to represent these remarks by means of numbers.

The *natural* tendency of population and wealth is to increase (the one by generation and the other by co-operative labor) according to the following progression:—

100;   200;   400;   800;   1600;   3200; etc.

The *actual* average increase of population is according to the following progression:—

Capitalists:	10;	12;	14;	16;	18;	20; etc.
Wagemen:	90;	108;	126;	144;	162;	180; etc.
Total	100;	120;	140;	160;	180;	200; etc.

The *actual* proportional difference between the increase of employed and unemployed wagemen is according to the following progression:—

Employed class:	89;	106;	123;	140;	157;	174; etc.
Unemployed:	1;	2;	3;	4;	5;	6; etc.

But there is a proportion which the repressive causes will never permit the pauper class to exceed: say about a fifth or a fourth. Beyond this, death is inexorably inflicted by all the means we have noted.

The *actual* average increase of wealth is according to the following progression:—

By numbers:	90;	100;	120;	150;	190;	240; etc.
By inventions:	+ 10;	+ 20;	+ 30;	+ 40;	+ 50;	+ 60; etc.
Total	100;	120;	150;	190;	240;	300; etc.

But of this progression of actual wealth, the *actual* share of the appropriators and wagemen *per capita* is according to the following ratio:—

The appropriators take:	90;	110;	140;	180;	230;	290; etc.
The wagemen are allowed:	10;	10;	10;	10;	10;	10; etc.
Total	100;	120;	150;	190;	240;	300; etc.

Observe that this ratio is *per capita;* and that the ratio of the wagemen is rarely above the minimum of subsistence.

In other words the capitalists get the wealth that should be divided among those who produce it, according to actual average labor-time.

Observe that when at any point the share of an appropriator is nine times greater than that of a wageman, at the next point it is ten times, and so on indefinitely.

5. Manifestly it is the right, as well as interest of labor to close up or at least diminish the capacity of the parasitic or intermediary draw-offs I have described; for every bit of capital is either (1) the free gift of God and therefore common property, without ransom being due to any person, or (2) it is value which labor alone has added to natural things, and so far, therefore, the rightful property of labor alone. To a *fundamental change of system* must, therefore, the world look for a restoration of the economic equilibrium; and there is no prospect of this but in one direction. If labor and capital were united in the same persons, and these were united by the law of love which is from our Lord Jesus Christ, there would be ABUNDANCE for all mankind.

Utopian Literature

AN ARNO PRESS/NEW YORK TIMES COLLECTION

Adams, Frederick Upham.
President John Smith; The Story of a Peaceful Revolution. 1897.

Bird, Arthur.
Looking Forward: A Dream of the United States of the Americas in 1999. 1899.

[Blanchard, Calvin.]
The Art of Real Pleasure. 1864.

Brinsmade, Herman Hine.
Utopia Achieved: A Novel of the Future. 1912.

Caryl, Charles W.
New Era. 1897.

Chavannes, Albert.
The Future Commonwealth. 1892.

Child, William Stanley.
The Legal Revolution of 1902. 1898.

Collens, T. Wharton.
Eden of Labor; or, The Christian Utopia. 1876.

Cowan, James.
Daybreak. A Romance of an Old World. 1896. 2nd ed.

Craig, Alexander.
Ionia; Land of Wise Men and Fair Women. 1898.

Daniel, Charles S.
AI: A Social Vision. 1892.

Devinne, Paul.
The Day of Prosperity: A Vision of the Century to Come. 1902.

Edson, Milan C.
Solaris Farm. 1900.

Fuller, Alvarado M.
A. D. 2000. 1890.

Geissler, Ludwig A.
Looking Beyond. 1891.

Hale, Edward Everett.
How They Lived in Hampton. 1888.

Hale, Edward Everett.
Sybaris and Other Homes. 1869.

Harris, W. S.
Life in a Thousand Worlds. 1905.

Henry, W. O.
Equitania. 1914.

Hicks, Granville, with Richard M. Bennett.
The First to Awaken. 1940.

Lewis, Arthur O., editor
American Utopias: Selected Short Fiction. 1790–1954.

McGrady, Thomas.
Beyond the Black Ocean. 1901.

Mendes H. Pereira.
Looking Ahead. 1899.

Michaelis, Richard.
Looking Further Forward. An Answer to
Looking Backward by Edward Bellamy. 1890.

Moore, David A.
The Age of Progress. 1856.

Noto, Cosimo.
The Ideal City. 1903.

Olerich, Henry.
A Cityless and Countryless World. 1893.

Parry, David M.
The Scarlet Empire. 1906.

Peck, Bradford.
The World a Department Store. 1900.

Reitmeister, Louis Aaron.
If Tomorrow Comes. 1934.

Roberts, J. W.
Looking Within. 1893.

Rosewater, Frank.
'96; A Romance of Utopia. 1894.

Satterlee, W. W.
Looking Backward and What I Saw. 2nd ed. 1890.

Schindler, Solomon.
Young West; A Sequel to Edward Bellamy's Celebrated
    Novel "Looking Backward." 1894.

Smith, Titus K.
Altruria. 1895.

Steere, C. A.
When Things Were Doing. 1908.

Taylor, William Alexander.
Intermere. 1901.

Thiusen, Ismar.
The Diothas, or, A Far Look Ahead. 1883.

Vinton, Arthur Dudley.
Looking Further Backward. 1890.

Wooldridge, C. W.
Perfecting the Earth. 1902.

Wright, Austin Tappan.
Islandia. 1942.